COUNSELING SERIES II: MARRIAGE

BOOK 3

MAINTAINING FAMILIAL RELATIONSHIPS

"This is a great mystery"

(Ephesians 5:32)

BISHOP YOUSSEF

ST MARY & MOSES ABBEY PRESS

Counseling Series II: Marriage — Book 3: Maintaining Familial Relationships

Designed & Published by:
St. Mary & St. Moses Abbey Press
101 S Vista Dr., Sandia, TX 78383
stmabbeypress.com

Cover design by Brigitte Iskander.

Library of Congress Control Number: 2021943857

Preface

This book is composed of several homilies and lectures by His Grace Bishop Youssef, the Bishop of the Coptic Orthodox Diocese of the Southern United States, over a period of twenty-nine years (1989–2018) on the subject of marriage.

In some cases, sections from different homilies and lectures were combined in order to minimize repetition as much as possible. However, because an attempt was also made to preserve the meaning and value of each homily and lecture, the reader may notice points that are repeated from chapter to chapter.

This book is the third book in a series of four books on Marriage and it provides guidance for how to maintain familial relationships. The last section of this book contains questions asked at the end of several homilies and lectures and His Grace's answers.

We pray that the Lord may bless your reading of this book, "the eyes of your understanding being enlightened,"[1] and guide us all on our search for "the wisdom that is from above."[2]

St. Mary & St. Phoebe Consecrated Sisters
Coptic Orthodox Diocese of the Southern United States

---

1   Eph 1:18
2   Jas 3:17

In the name of the Father,
and of the Son,
and of the Holy Spirit,
one God.
Amen.

Table of Contents

Part I
COMMUNICATION

---

1 Communication

Communication Channels
Verbal Communication

Nonverbal Communication

Communication Styles
Formal Communication

Informal Communication

Communication and Behavior
Aggressive Communication

Passive Communication

Passive-Aggressive Communication

Assertive Communication

Gender Differences in Communication

Communication is the process that involves the exchange of information, thoughts, ideas, and emotions. We are always communicating, either with ourselves, God, or one another. There are three elements in communication:

1. The sender: The person who initiates communication.
2. The receiver: The person on the other end.
3. The communication channel: The channel through which communication occurs, such as email or the telephone.

There is a simple rule about communication that states, "You cannot *not* communicate." Even if you decide that you are not going to talk to someone and end all communication with this person, you are still sending a message that you are upset. Whether you are speaking or silent, you are always communicating.

We engage in a variety of behaviors when we communicate with one another, and we will look at many of them. It would be very helpful for you to examine your own style of communication and understand how you express yourself and how you communicate with others. The appropriate choice of behavior is vitally important if we are to communicate effectively.

Communication Channels

Various aspects of communication can be organized into different groupings. The first aspect is the communication channel, which can be verbal or nonverbal.

Verbal Communication

Verbal communication can be oral or written. Oral communication refers to spoken words. It can occur face to face, over the telephone, or through voice chat on the Internet. This type of communication is influenced by the tone of voice, pitch, volume, speed, and clarity. For example, I can speak slowly or quickly; I can yell or speak softly.

9

Written communication, such as letters or email, is influenced by the style of writing, vocabulary, clarity, and precision of language. Written communication is often not as clear as oral communication. Because of this, we do not encourage using written communication at the beginning of a relationship, for example, between an engaged couple. We do not encourage them to talk often using email or online chats because many misunderstandings may occur, especially due to the absence of facial expression and the inability to read the other person's feelings. A sentence may be understood in many ways. Moreover, some people may use very confusing words that can be understood in different ways. This is similar to politicians, whose words and sentences can be understood and interpreted in many ways.

Nonverbal Communication

Nonverbal communication refers to body language and includes posture, hand gestures, and bodily movements. For example, when a family meets with me in my office, I pay attention to the way they are sitting. If the wife sits far away from her husband, I can sense that the boundaries between them are rigid. If they sit next to each other, I can sense that the boundaries are elastic. I also observe their hand gestures, and if they avoid looking at each other. All of these things are important in understanding family dynamics and the pattern of communication in the household.

Nonverbal communication also includes facial expressions. Facial expressions can vary from culture to culture. For example, consider eye contact. In certain cultures, eye contact can be interpreted as boldness, but in other cultures, avoiding eye contact may be interpreted as disinterest. Thus, nonverbal expression has to be interpreted within the context of culture.

Nonverbal communication also includes signs, photographs, sketches, paintings, and pictures. Emotions and feelings can be expressed via nonverbal communication. When the rich young ruler told the Lord Jesus Christ that he had been keeping the commandments from his youth, we read that, "Jesus, looking at him, loved him" (Mk 10:21). The Lord did not say, "Good job! I love you." However, everyone was able to read the love in His eyes. Thus, nonverbal communication can communicate emotions and feelings from one person to another.

Communication Styles

A second aspect of communication is the style and purpose, which can be formal or informal.

Formal Communication

With formal communication, we use an official format, which is what is used in business interactions or between strangers. When you meet someone for the first time, you interact in a formal manner and are not immediately friendly. This is straightforward, official, precise communication. Usually, there is no emotion in formal communication; it is strict and rigid.

Informal Communication

Informal communication is free and unrestrained, and occurs more often between friends and family members. People speak with ease and let their guard down. There are no rules or guidelines. You are able to communicate and share whatever thought comes to mind. This kind of communication does not necessarily have boundaries on time, place, or subject; we can talk about any subject, anywhere, at any time.

Communication and Behavior

The most important category of communication methods is that which is based on behavior. Communication can be divided into four types based on behavior. Each one of us should examine which of the four is his predominate behavior in communication.

Aggressive Communication

In aggressive communication, the aggressor places his rights above the rights of the other person, and refuses to take responsibility. Aggression usually involves manipulation. The aggressor attempts to make people do what he wants. He uses many ways to manipulate the other person, either by inducing guilt, intimidation, or by using a control tactic such as anger. Aggressive communication never works in a relationship. In fact, it destroys relationships. It is sometimes referred to as verbal or emotional abuse. Aggressive communication hurts, offends, and isolates the other person's rights and feelings, because the aggressor is only focused on what he or she wants.

Fear or insecurity can cause people to revert to aggressive communication. If someone is insecure, he may cover this up by using aggression to gain control. Insecurity is a feeling of not having control over a situation, so the person tries to gain control over the situation either through manipulation or anger, i.e., aggression. Lack of self-esteem or self-confidence can also cause someone to communicate aggressively. Unfortunately, aggressive communication is very common in Egyptian culture. People frequently yell and curse at each other and at children.

Passive Communication

Passive communication can be divided into two types. The first type is called *submissive* or *accommodating* and is based on compliance. With this type, a person agrees to everything, approves of everything, and always submits. He wants to please others, even at the expense of his opinion. He thinks that it is okay to ignore his opinions or his rights. If he disagrees with someone or says no to someone, he may feel guilty or have anxiety. In order for him to overcome his anxiety, false sense of guilt, or fear, he allows his thoughts or views to be ignored and allows the other person to take advantage of him. In other words, he chooses to ignore his rights in order to reduce his anxiety, sense of guilt, or fear.

Parents may sometimes raise their children to be compliant

or submissive in a negative way. For example, the parents may be controlling and not allow their children to disagree with them; if the children disagree, they get punished. Thus, the children become fearful and develop anxiety. They may also make the children feel guilty: "Is this how you talk to your father?" "Is this the way to deal with your mother, after everything I have done for you?"

Thus, this behavior is instilled in children by parents, teachers, or other authority figures. A person suppresses his opinions and feelings, and just lets things go. Someone who pleases or accommodates others actually senses an immediate feeling of pleasure after doing so because he put the other person at ease. Because of this, some people develop an addiction to this style, despite the fact that St. Paul says, "If I still pleased men, I would not be a bondservant of Christ" (Gal 1:10). There are times when one needs to take a stand, and times when one needs to ask God. Yes, many times we need to sacrifice our rights for others, but there should be a clear message from God that He wants me to do so. In other situations, one must stand for the truth.

Someone who is accommodating and submissive does not want to say no even to unreasonable requests. He may not want to draw attention to himself because he does not feel as good as others. He has an inferiority complex and feels that his opinions may not be beneficial. For example, if he is sitting with a group of people, he may not participate in the discussion because he feels that his opinions are not as good as other peoples' opinions. Someone who wants to be pleasing does not speak much, questions very little, and does very little. He always says, "Okay, that is fine, no problem," even if internally he is not at ease. For him, it is safer not to react and better to disappear than to stand up and be noticed.

We sometimes confuse inferiority with humility, but there is a big difference between the two. A humble person knows that he is nothing but also knows that he can do everything through the Lord Jesus Christ who strengthens him (see Phil 4:13). A humble person has self-confidence, which comes from his trust in the Lord. He has healthy self-esteem because he knows the Lord abides in him. However, inferiority is the sense that everybody else is better; they

13

are inferior to everybody, and that is it. There is no sense of God-given talent or the existence of God within them. They do not feel that they can do all things through Christ who strengthens them. When parents and Sunday school teachers teach their children humility, they need to keep this balance. Otherwise, we will raise a generation of children lacking in the virtue of humility but with inferiority complexes.

Someone may constantly seek approval and recognition from others and may, therefore, communicate in this passive method in order for everyone to love and praise him. We sometimes label people who voice their opinions as troublemakers, so people may choose this style in order to appear excessively polite and helpful. They go beyond their ability just to please others. They are what we call *people-pleasers*. In St. Paul's first letter to the Thessalonians, he considered pleasing others a sin (see 1 Thess 2:4), because many times we please others at the expense of the truth and we justify it by saying that we do not want any conflicts.

Over the years, a person who uses this style of communication will accumulate resentment, especially within a family. For example, if a wife always gives up her rights, resentment will amass within her over the years. Eventually, her style of communication will go from being passive and submissive, to aggressive. She will suddenly start getting upset and yelling because she can no longer contain her emotions.

The second type of passive communication is based on avoidance. These people try to avoid confrontation or making a scene at all costs. Avoidance can take many different forms. For example, a person can leave a discussion and go in his room and close the door. Men are better at avoidance. As soon as there is a discussion they do not like, they just get up and leave. Another way to avoid a discussion is quickly agreeing to whatever is said. Agreeing does not mean that he will do what he says; he just wants to end the discussion, and he will most likely *not* do what he says. Having a discussion or a confrontation may mean that he needs to change or compromise, but he may not want to do either of those things. He ignores his responsibilities because he does not wish to be bothered by the consequences. Thus, he avoids confrontation in order to avoid responsibility.

As people can become addicted to pleasing and accommodating others, people can also become addicted to, and very skillful in, avoiding any uncomfortable situation. They do this either by refusing to recognize the problem ("You are making it into a bigger problem than it is. There is really no problem"), or by avoiding any confrontational situation.

Avoidance can be displayed in many ways. For example, not answering phone calls from certain people—if he sees her number, he does not answer and says that he was busy—or refusing to socialize in a certain place, or refusing to share certain information. For example, he tells his wife certain things, but eliminates other things, such as what his salary is, what their finances are like, his plans, or what he did that day. He intentionally does not share any information in order to avoid any sort of confrontation. If she asks him how he is doing, he responds by simply saying, "Fine, thank God," and that is the end of the discussion. These people make elaborate plans in order to avoid any confrontation or communication. He thinks about everything she may possibly say and how he will respond, and develops a plan in order to avoid communicating.

Passive-Aggressive

The third kind, passive-aggressive, is a combination of the first two. In this case, a person avoids direct confrontation, but tries to send indirect messages to hurt or manipulate the other person. He attempts to get even through manipulation. He does not directly confront the other person, and, at the same time, he attempts to retaliate in conflict through manipulation or aggression. If someone upsets him, he may start to think that this person needs to be taught a lesson. He thinks about how to make him suffer indirectly, and how to punish him indirectly, without confronting him. If someone begins to think this way, this person is heading toward the passive-aggressive style of communication. He sends hidden messages, makes the other person suffer, or hurts the other person.

Assertive Communication

The last kind is called assertive communication. This is the most effective and healthiest form of communication, but, unfortunately, it is used the least often. The Lord urged us to use assertive communication when He said, "If your brother sins against you, go and tell him his fault between you and him alone" (Mt 18:15). He did not say to avoid him, to be aggressive toward him, or to send him hidden messages to discipline or punish him. Many people say that they do not like to confront others, but this is because we do not know how to do it. If we confront others correctly, it will produce results in most cases; the Lord said, "*If* he hears you, you have gained your brother" (Mt 18:15, emphasis added), so there is a possibility confrontation will not bring forth results.

We need to learn to be objective, to have reconciliation be our goal, to take responsibility for our mistakes, and to be ready to forgive and accept forgiveness. If we learn how to confront others in a healthy way, how to communicate in an assertive way, and improve our communication skills, this will heal many wounds in family relationships.

In order to be able to communicate assertively, you need to have intact self-esteem. A humble person has self-confidence and healthy self-esteem because he knows and feels that he can do all things in Jesus Christ who strengthens him. His confidence is based in his relationship with God. Thus, he has an intact self-esteem and self-confidence to communicate without manipulation and to send messages clearly.

In assertive communication, there is compromise from both parties, and both try to reach a mutually satisfying solution. A workable compromise is often the best solution that is accepted by both parties. If I refuse to compromise, this means I am aggressive and want things to be done my way only. Moreover, in assertive communication, needs are expressed clearly and forthrightly. Sometimes, if one spouse needs something from the other, instead of telling her, he becomes frustrated and angry. There are two big communication problems in Egyptian culture. Most of us do not know how to express our needs, because we feel that is weakness, and we do not know how to express our negative emotions when we are hurt. These are the two areas we need to improve in. Because of this, we sometimes resort to hidden messages, indirect methods of communication, or manipulation in order to get what we want. However, it would be better to clearly state what you need.

Assertive communication relies on honest, direct, and appropriate expression of needs, wants, or feelings as a first, and not a last, resort. One of the best descriptions of communication is found in the Book of Genesis about Adam in Eve: "They were both naked, the man and his wife, and were not ashamed" (Gen 2:25). We do not interpret this to refer solely to physical nakedness, but to the ability to uncover all one's thoughts, ideas, fears, needs, hurts, and wishes without the fear of being ashamed or rejected. What makes a person cover up his needs or his weak areas? It is the fear of rejection. One person is scared to share information with the other person and be rejected. Mutual acceptance leads to more open, fruitful, and healthy communication. St. Paul says, "Receive one another" (Rom 15:7). Therefore, this is the ideal model for communication that God used in creating Adam and Eve, but, unfortunately, it was lost immediately after the fall, and they began to cover up in front of one another.

People who care about their relationships and strive for "win-win" situations use assertive communication. In win-win situations, *both* people leave satisfied; there is no loser. With assertive communication, a person respects his boundaries as well as the boundaries of others. If I allow others to push me beyond my boundaries, I will accumulate resentment in my heart and eventually become aggressive toward them. True assertive behavior involves protecting your space and rights while not isolating others' space and rights. In aggressive communication, I protect my space and my rights, but I ignore those of others. With passive communication, I allow the other person to take advantage of me and disregard my space and my rights. Assertive communication respects the space and rights of both parties.

Gender Differences in Communication

Understanding gender differences in communication helps us communicate in a healthy way. This information is based on numerous research on the attitudes men and women have when they communicate. Women tend to see the importance of communication and enjoy talking more than men. The female self grows in relationships, while the male self grows independently, which is why females value communication more than males. Research shows that on average, a woman will speak 6000 words per day, whereas a man only speaks 2000 words per day. The numbers can vary from culture to culture and from person to person, but the consistent finding is that women generally speak three to four times more words per day than men.

Another important difference is that men's conversations are based mostly on facts, while women look for facts, emotions, and anything else that could possibly be said. We see this in confession. A man comes to confession, mentions his sins in three to four minutes, and is finished. On the other hand, when a woman confesses, it may take her thirty minutes to finally get to her first sin.

An interesting point is that both males and females want the other gender to be like them, which is unfair. If a man expects his wife to say just the facts, this is an incorrect expectation, and if she expects him to talk about his emotions and feelings, this also is an incorrect expectation. Because of this, everything a man does makes sense to other men, and everything a woman does makes sense to other women.

The problem is that men do not always understand women's style of communication, and women do not always understand the men's style. This is why miscommunication occurs. We either cannot understand how the other communicates, or we do not *want* to know so we intentionally refuse to understand. Usually, it is a combination of the two. We say we were brought up to understand our own style, and we do not take the time or put in the effort to learn about anyone else. However, if we take the time to learn about the opposite gender, understand one another, and try to compromise, life will be much easier. We need to make the effort to learn about other people's ways. This will help us get what we want, avoid conflict, and have healthy, long-lasting relationships.

Many aspects of communication come down to how things are said, and not what is said, i.e., how the message is communicated and not the content of the message. We can send clear messages without saying a word, but simply through body language. We can alter the meaning of a message by changing the emphasis or our tone of voice. It is important to acquire a coherent pattern of voice, speech, content, and facial expression. All of these things together must communicate the same message, if we want to convey our intended behavior clearly.

Try to evaluate your style of communication. Which one of the four behaviors do you use most often? Do you feel comfortable or uncomfortable with this behavior? It would be a problem if, for example, you are aggressive, or you are passive, and you feel comfortable with it. This would mean that you are addicted to this style of communication, and it would require determination and grace from God to change it.

2 Effective Communication

The Definition of Good Communication

The Importance of Good Communication

Types of Communication

"Instrumental" and "Affective" Communication

Clear or Masked and Direct or Indirect Communication

Judas Iscariot

Miscommunication in the Holy Bible

Fifteen Tips for Effective Communication

Communicating with God

Communication in the Service

The Definition of Good Communication

Communication is about being able to express our thoughts as well as our emotions. Effective communication entails being able to understand the messages I receive. In order to communicate well, we must be able to understand what others are saying as well as the emotions with which they are speaking. For example, if someone is leaving the house, he may say, "I am going out now." This can be said in many different ways. He may state it factually, indicating that he is going to do some activity. Or, he may say it with negative emotion, meaning that he is upset. Thus, you need to pay attention not only to the content of the message, but also to how the message is expressed.

Communication involves active listening as well as speaking. Often, and especially when we argue, the listener begins preparing his response while the speaker is talking. Consequently, the listener does not pay attention to the speaker. This happens frequently in family counseling sessions. For example, if the husband is speaking and the wife wants to interrupt him and respond, I ask her, "Can you tell me what he just said?" In many cases, they cannot tell you what their spouse said because they were not listening; they were preparing their response. If we do this, we will never become active listeners. This is why you should paraphrase in your own words what the other person said before you begin to speak. For example, after listening to your spouse, you would say, "Okay, you mean such and such." Doing this gives the other person the message that he or she is heard and understood.

The Importance of Good Communication

Effective communication within the family is important for many reasons. First, it enables us to express our needs, feelings, and concerns to one another. Many of us have a problem expressing our needs. We consider doing so a weakness. This is why we often use indirect communication and make the other person guess what we need, which leads to many assumptions. There is nothing wrong with expressing your needs. The Lord Jesus Christ Himself expressed His needs and said to Peter, James, and John, "Stay here and watch with Me" (Mt 26:38). It is as if He was expressing that He needed them to stay awake with Him on the night He was getting ready for the cross. Good and effective communication enables each person to express his needs, feelings, and concerns with precision.

It also allows family members to express their differences. A husband and wife are two different people in gender, education, spirituality, upbringing, etc. Thus, it is normal for a family to have disagreements. We expect disagreement but not conflict; they should know how to resolve their conflicts. For example, when a church board tells me that they have never disagreed about anything, I have many questions regarding whether this committee is functioning correctly or not. It is impossible for six people to never disagree. Either they are very passive and say yes to everything to make it easy on themselves, or there is no room to freely express their opinions. Differences increase our love for one another. Through effective communication, we try to work out conflicts in spite of our differences.

Third, effective communication is a channel for expressing love and admiration for one another. All of us need to be loved and admired. Many people say, "We are too old for things like this. I do not know how to say such words." However, everyone needs to hear words of love and encouragement. St. Paul says to Timothy, "Let the elders who rule well be counted worthy of double honor" (1 Tim 5:17). "Elders" in this verse means priests, so this is even a need in the service. St. Paul also frequently mentions encouragement in his epistles, and encourages his children and the congregation. The Lord Jesus Christ Himself encouraged others. When Peter said, "You are the Christ, the Son of the living God," the Lord told him, "Blessed are you, Simon Bar-Jonah, for flesh and blood has not revealed this to you" (Mt 16:16–17). Words of love and encouragement must be communicated because this is a need.

[Please refer to Chapter 8 for more on encouragement.]

Therefore, effective communication helps us resolve the unavoidable problems that arise in every family, express our needs, share our differences, and communicate our love and admiration to one another. Research has found that when there is good communication, the family is healthy and functional, and there is marital satisfaction. In other words, satisfaction is higher when communication is better. Many family problems are caused by miscommunication. Poor communication can be described as *indirect* and *unclear*. Poor communication in itself, and not the differences between the husband and wife, can cause many problems, such as excessive family conflict, ineffective problem solving, lack of intimacy, behavioral problems in the children, lack of satisfaction in the relationship, and weak emotional bonding.

There was a study done on young children in which they found that if parents give two contradictory messages to their children, the child does something called *disassociation* in order to reconcile the contradictory messages. This may cause the child to develop Schizophrenia and/or Dissociative Identity Disorder. For example, a father is upset and yells at his son, but tells him, "I love you!" His facial expression does not say that he loves him, so the son receives two contradictory messages: The father says that he loves him, but his actions do not show this love, and attempting to reconcile the two contradictory messages could cause the child to develop a psychiatric disorder.

Types of Communication

"Instrumental" and "Affective" Communication

There are two types of communication within the family: "instrumental" and "affective." Instrumental communication refers to task-orientated communication; the family members communicate in order to accomplish a specific goal for the family or share facts. For example, they may discuss what kind of school the children will attend, buying a house together, refinancing a loan, or money management, or share facts such as, "I am going out now." Affective communication refers to how family members communicate their emotions and feelings with one another. Examples include saying, "I am sad," "I am upset," "I am happy," "I love," etc. Many people function very well with instrumental communication but have great

23

difficulty with affective communication. Also, we sometimes know how to express our negative feelings, but not our positive feelings. Feelings of love and emotion may weaken as time passes and consequently, the expression of those feelings also weakens. Healthy families are able to communicate well in both areas: sharing facts as well as acknowledging, validating, and expressing feelings toward others.

Clear or Masked and Direct or Indirect Communication

Communication can be clear or masked, and direct or indirect. Clear communication means that the message is clear. If someone is upset about something, he says, "I am upset about this particular behavior." There is no room for assumption here. Masked communication is when the message is vague. For example, someone says, "I am upset," and when asked why, he says, "I do not know; there are just many things bothering me."

Direct communication is when someone directs his feelings toward a specific person: "I am upset with *you*" or "I am happy with *you*." Indirect communication is when the message is not directed to the person for whom it is intended. Here, the person simply makes a comment and leaves everyone to understand it however they take it. For example, because a husband is upset with his wife, he would say, "All women do such and such."

From these four techniques, we get four styles of communication: clear and direct, clear and indirect, masked and direct, or masked and indirect. Of course, the best kind of communication is clear and direct. We will look at an example of each type in order to better understand them. Let us say that a father is upset with his son because it is his son's responsibility to take out the trash and he did not do it. If the father is using clear and direct communication, he would say, "Son, I am disappointed that you forgot to take out the trash today without me having to remind you." He is talking to his son and at the same time he told him exactly why he is upset. There is no room for assumption. However, clear and indirect communication would be that the father does not direct the message to his son but makes it clear that he is upset: "It is disappointing when people forget to do their chores." This message is about people in general, and not directed to his son. The son may not understand that the father is referring to him, but the father expects his son to understand, apologize, or fix his behavior. This is the drawback of indirect communication.

The third style is masked and direct. The father will direct his words to his son but he will not say exactly why he is upset: "Son, people just do not work as hard as they should anymore." Since he does not say what he is referring to, the son may not get the message. With masked and indirect communication, which is the worst type, he would say something like, "Youth today are very lazy." This is just a very general comment; no one would be able to understand its relevance.

Communication needs to be clear and direct, also referred to as *assertive* communication. Most of us are afraid of confrontation or avoid it. We often use either masked or indirect communication, assuming and expecting the other person to understand or guess what we mean. However, as the Holy Bible says, "How shall they hear without a preacher?" (Rom 10:14), meaning how will he know without you telling him? Moreover, we sometimes use this technique in confession and expect our confession father[3] to detect the sin and understand what we want to say. When we are clear in our confessions, we will receive good advice as well as victory over sin. Revealing a thought weakens its power. When I am fought by a thought and confess it clearly, this will weaken the power of that thought.

Judas Iscariot

In the service, we find that when someone hides something from his parents and his confession father, he eventually gets into many problems. For example, if a youth is considering suicide and hides this thought from his parents, his confession father, or any of his

---

3   A priest to whom one regularly confesses. This is the common practice in the Coptic Orthodox Church.

friends, he will eventually take his own life. However, if he shares that he is upset and feels hopeless and is thinking about committing suicide, we can help him. People who express that they are in such a situation receive help and can overcome the lack of hope in their lives.

In light of this, I started thinking about Judas Iscariot. I have a personal meditation about him. What would have happened if he had shared his thoughts with Peter, Andrew, John, or James, if there had been clear and direct communication and he had told them, "I really regret what I did. How could I have delivered the Lord? I feel there can be no forgiveness for me. I am going to commit suicide and end my life!" I imagine that if he had revealed his thoughts clearly and directly to one of the other disciples, things would not have ended the way they did. Most likely, the disciples would have reminded him about how the Lord forgave the woman caught in adultery (Jn 8:2–11) and the woman who came to Simon's house (Lk 7:36–50). They would have also reminded him about the Lord's love and how He said, "The one who comes to Me I will by no means cast out" (Jn 6:37). Peter would have told him, "I am like you. I denied Him, but I have hope in His love. When He looked at me while I was denying Him, His expression was reprimanding but also full of love, acceptance, and forgiveness. That is why I have faith that God will accept me." Judas's life could have changed. However, he refused to communicate. He refused to reveal his thoughts clearly and directly, and he lost his life on earth as well as in heaven. This illustrates the importance of clear and direct communication with family members and confession fathers. Revealing thoughts weakens their power.

Miscommunication in the Holy Bible

An example of miscommunication in the Holy Bible occurred between Isaac and Rebekah. At one point, God told Rebekah, "Two nations are in your womb ... and the older shall serve the younger" (Gen 25:23). Did Rebekah share this with Isaac? The Holy Bible did not say. However, I expect that if Rebekah *had* shared this with Isaac, he would not have decided to bless Esau, his firstborn son, against

God's commandment. This is why we can assume that Rebekah probably failed to communicate to Isaac that God told her the older would serve the younger. The same applies when Isaac asked Esau to come be blessed. Isaac spoke to Esau, and Rebekah *overheard* the dialogue between them, so there was no communication between the husband and wife. He did not tell her what he was planning to do with Esau. Perhaps if he had started a discussion with her, she may have said, "No, how can we do this? God said that the older will serve the younger," and they would have discussed it.

Moreover, Rebekah avoided confrontation. She did not go to Isaac and tell him, "What are you doing? This is not what God commanded." Instead, she decided to solve the problem in an indirect way. She asked Jacob to go hunting and told him that she would prepare food for his father, etc. Basically, she devised a plan in order to avoid confrontation. Instead of going to talk to Isaac, she was deceptive. Many times, we do this. The deception was successful at first and Jacob received the blessing, but then hatred developed between Esau and Jacob. Esau wanted to kill Jacob, and Jacob fled to his uncle and stayed there for almost twenty years. A *major* conflict occurred between Esau and Jacob, mainly because of a lack of communication. If Isaac and Rebekah had clearly discussed their plans together and decided what they were going to do regarding the blessing, things would not have gone so far. This is an example of how poor communication between parents can lead to major conflict even between the children. When spouses do not communicate as a couple, the children often pay the price. God, in His love, can indeed bring "out of the eater ... something to eat" (Judg 14:14), and He fixes our mistakes and transforms them to good, but this does not mean that we should continue in our mistakes.

Fifteen Tips for Effective Communication

1. Communicate frequently. If you want to master anything, you need to practice. Communication is a skill and any skill needs training. Do not just say that you know how to communicate. You need to train yourself. Being good

communicators does not simply happen. "So then, my beloved brethren, let every man be swift to hear, slow to speak, slow to wrath" (Jas 1:19). Being swift to hear means to understand; it is not just listening to the words. Be slow to speak because you need to understand before you speak. Be slow to wrath because there is no place for anger in communication. Use any opportunity for dialogue. One barrier to effective communication is being too busy and not having the time. [Please refer to Chapter 3 for more on the barriers to effective communication.] It is very important to have frequent communication with your spouse, your children, and your family. Talking to one another will help us get closer and get to know each other better. Barriers form when we avoid discussions.

2. Be an active listener when someone else is talking. Do not simply listen; actively listen. Pay attention. Sometimes, when someone is talking to us, we are too busy thinking of a response that we do not focus on what the person is saying. Try to really understand what is in the other person's heart. What is the real message they want to convey? Try to be objective as much as possible. Do not understand the other person subjectively. Do not try to understand through your own eyes and perspective, but understand them as they really are. Many times, we misinterpret what others say because of our own perceptions. Our perceptions can cause us to hear what we want to hear and block what we want to reject. Many times, we have good intentions, but we cannot express them correctly. If we trust one another, we should not just jump to conclusions and make quick judgments about the other person. Through active listening, exploring, and questioning we can understand the other person precisely. Learning to listen is more important than learning to express yourself directly and clearly. Active listening involves the following:

a. Try your best to understand the other person's point of view, even if you do not agree with it. There is a difference between understanding and agreeing. For example, I can understand why thieves steal. I can understand why terrorists attacked America on September 11th. I understand their point of view, but this does not mean that I agree.

You may need to paraphrase what you heard to make sure that you understood it correctly. If the message is not clear, there is nothing wrong with asking, "What do you mean? Would you please elaborate?" When the Lord Jesus Christ told the parable of the sower, the disciples did not understand and asked Him to explain it to them.4 When they asked, they learned and benefited.

Some people communicate vaguely on purpose; they rarely give clear messages. This is most likely to avoid being caught in a mistake or because they do not want to take responsibility for what they are saying. I know someone who usually only tells half the story, and I always tell him this. I have to ask about twenty questions in order to understand.

b. Pay close attention to the verbal as well as nonverbal messages. Nonverbal messages can communicate that the other person is angry, upset, and disappointed. Pay attention to facial expressions and body language. These send signals.

Sometimes, when I visit a family, I can get an idea about them from the way they are sitting—who is sitting next to whom. This is especially true if there is a problem between them. In this case, you may find, for example, the son and the father sitting to one side and the mother and the daughter sitting on the other. This shows me that the there is a problem between the father and the mother and that the son

---

4   Cf. Matthew 13:3-23; Mark 4:3-20; Luke 8:5-13.

is taking the father's side while the daughter is on the mother's side. However, this works up to a certain point. You cannot make a judgment from nonverbal communication alone, but when you compare the verbal and nonverbal messages, this gives you greater understanding of the other person's point of view.

c. Acknowledge and respect the other person's perspective even if it is different from yours. You can be understanding and respectful, and also disagree. However, do not belittle the other person's message. Do not tell him that what he is saying is nonsense. Naturally, a comment like this puts a barrier between the spouses. It causes a fear of rejection and makes the other person not want to talk.

In a Christian family, each person should be able to express his or her point of view freely without ever being ashamed, no matter what their opinion is. There should be no fear that what I say can later be used against me, or will not be respected. Respecting others' different points of view is fundamental in effective family communication. If someone belittles another person's message, this hurts. We need to know how to respect the other person's perspective and opinion.

d. Do not interrupt each other. However, some spouses tend to talk all the time, so if the advice is followed to not interrupt each other, he or she may speak for hours. Start by deciding that each person will talk for a set time, e.g., five minutes, without interruption. The first person will speak for five minutes without interruption; then, the other person will respond. Before you respond, first repeat back what he or she said and summarize it in order to be sure that you understand exactly what the other person meant to convey. Then, say what you want to say. After five minutes, the other person will speak again, etc.

3. Be open and honest with one another, speaking the truth to one another, as St. Paul says in Ephesians 4:15. We need to learn how to speak the truth in love. It does not work if you tell someone that everything is fine, while inside you are angry with him. There will be no trust between you. Openness and honesty build trust between the family members. What do you think the trust between Isaac and Rebekah was like after Isaac realized that it was Rebekah who had encouraged Jacob to deceive him? I am sure the trust was shaken. Isaac would have felt that Rebekah deceived him and also encouraged her son to deceive him. Imagine two people living together without trust. Many family problems arise because of lack of trust. Without trust, family members cannot build strong relationships. When there is clear and direct communication, this creates trust between family members and trust strengthens the ties between them and binds them together. Even if they differ, each one knows that the other will not be deceptive. I hope that we can learn how to communicate our feelings, needs, emotions, and disappointments in an open and clear way. [Please refer to Chapter 4 for more on trust in the family.]

In true marital unity, both the husband and the wife are able to express and uncover their feelings without fear or shame. Thus, if fear of expressing oneself exists, it is important to find out why. Maybe there is some sort of invalidation or belittling of the other person's feelings. If someone feels secure enough to express and share his feelings, he or she will definitely share them. Insecurity is what causes us to put our guard up and become defensive all the time. If the other person has difficulty expressing his or her feelings, we need to create a safe and secure atmosphere in order to facilitate this process.

When our Lord Jesus Christ was expecting the three disciples to stay awake and watch with Him, and they did not,

He said to them, "Could you not watch with Me one hour?" (Mt 26:40). He showed that He was upset. He then showed them that He understood their perspective by saying that He knows "The spirit indeed is willing, but the flesh is weak" (Mt 26:41). Also, He communicated to Peter that he would deny Him three times before the rooster crows (see Mt 26:34).

4. When you communicate with family members, you must take the circumstances, background, and age of each person into consideration. Think about the person with whom you are communicating. Not everyone understands nor judges situations in the same way you do. You come from a different family and upbringing than your wife. Some people are conservative, and some people are liberal, to an extent that is appropriate for us as Christians and children of God. There are people who are extroverts, and love to socialize, and there are people who are introverts and more often prefer to be alone. When I understand the other person and how he views life, this will prevent me from attacking him with offensive words and comments. For example, if a wife is social and her husband does not like to go out a lot and prefers to stay in his office or at home all the time, he may continually offend her with hurtful words about how she is never home. She also may attack him and accuse him of always staying home, doing nothing, and having no friends. However, if each of them understood the other person's perspective and preferences, this would help them compromise. They would learn to sacrifice and meet in the middle. In this way, both of them would be comfortable.

The same applies when dealing with children and youth. Keep in mind that not all family members communicate in the same manner or at the same level, especially young children. Keep age difference and maturity level in mind. Listen carefully to what the children are saying, without making unwanted assumptions, and look at things from their perspective. Dealing with a young child is different from dealing with a teenager or an adult, but many parents believe that their children should behave like adults. That is not a correct expectation. For example, a father gives his child an allowance and the child uses it to buy a toy. The father considers a toy unimportant and he believes the child should use the money in a different way. However, for the child, this toy is more important than anything else.

You need to understand the child or the teenager's world, especially since we have two cultures in our families. Parents of children who grew up in the United States may have different points of view than their children. What the children are exposed to in elementary, middle, or high school in the United States is different from what you were exposed to in the same school years in Egypt. You should be cognizant about these differences when you talk to them. Otherwise, your expectations will impractical. Many youth say, "Dad does not understand me," and, "No one understands me in my house." Sometimes, they are right! Sometimes the parents live in a different world, not in the world in which our children are living. Can you imagine and understand everything that they are exposed to in school and with friends? Our youth are exposed to so many things, whereas we were not exposed to even 1% of these things. Therefore, in order to be able to communicate effectively, you need to fully understand the culture and the circumstances to which they are exposed.

We need to show them that we understand their point of view, even if it is wrong. If a youth tells me an opinion, and I disagree with that opinion, I should tell still him that I understand his perspective: "From your point of view, you are saying such and such." If I do this, he will say, "At least my parents understand me," or "Finally, His Grace and Abouna5 understand me." However, if we do not understand their perspective and attack them, they will say that no one understands them or feels for them.

Another example is that all of us like the church to be noiseless. We go to church to pray and usually it is peaceful. If a young child starts to scream or cry and his mother quickly gathers her things so she can leave with him, in those three

---

5   Abouna is a word in the Arabic language that means "our father" and refers to a priest.

or four minutes, people start staring at her, adding to her feelings of embarrassment. This young child is not aware that he is in church, and it is normal for young children to cry. However, sometimes we do not understand the circumstances others are enduring. Who knows—maybe when we were children, we also cried and caused noise in church as well? Do not misunderstand me; I am not encouraging noise in the church, but I encourage being understanding toward others and their situations, and helping them. Those looks are very hurtful and cause embarrassment. Many mothers refuse to attend the liturgy because of those stares, and say that they will attend again when their children grow up. Until then, they bring their children at the end of the liturgy so they can take communion. People do not look at the maturity level and age of these children, or at the mother's circumstances, and by their gazes they cause great embarrassment to mothers while they are attending church. Understanding other peoples' circumstances is a fundamental principle for effective communication.

5. Do not force others to speak with you at a certain time. If the other person is tired, exhausted, or just returning from work, be sensitive to this. There are people who insist on speaking at a certain time, without any consideration of the circumstances. This causes communication to fail. If I am not ready to listen but you start talking, how can we communicate? The Lord Jesus Christ told His disciples that if they entered a city to preach and the people did not receive them, to leave that city and not even take the city's dust that clings to their sandals with them (see Mt 10:14). You cannot force someone to listen to you, even if it is the word of God. You cannot force someone to hear God's word against his will. Respect the other person's desire to listen or not to listen.

If the husband loves soccer and he is completely focused on watching a game, and his wife comes in to talk about an important topic, he may say, "Okay, yes, I agree" in order to end the discussion. Of course, this is wrong timing; he is not listening or paying attention. If what you want to say is

34

important, do not say it at a time when the other person is not listening to you. Be sure that your spouse or the other person is listening. You can ask, "There is something I want to talk about. Is this a good time for us to talk?"

This sometimes happens with the priests. For example, after the Divine Liturgy when there is a long line waiting to greet the priest and take the blessed bread6, peoples sometimes choose this time to talk to Abouna about a big problem or an important issue. Abouna would be greeting everyone while trying to listen to the person who wants to talk to him. If the topic is important to you, choose a suitable time to share it with Abouna. Do not choose a time when he is distracted.

Sometimes, we have an urge to fix a situation immediately. If someone is angry about something, one spouse may tell the other or children that they must talk right now. If the other person is tired and requests to talk later, he still insists that they must talk immediately. Most likely, if the discussion takes place under this condition, it will not be effective and will end in conflict. Therefore, it is better to postpone it until the other person is ready. On the other hand, there are people who are avoidant; they will never be ready to talk, which makes the person pursuing the discussion frustrated. Every time he tries to talk, he is told, "Not now, this is not the right time. Let us postpone it for now." If you are an avoidant person, do not constantly refuse. You need to set a specific time. Say, for example, "I am not ready right now but can we talk about this in two days, after dinner?" It is better to assign a date and time so that you know when you will talk. The other person will not feel that you are just trying to avoid the topic. Setting another time for the discussion, one when you are both calm, is better for both parties in order to solve the problem.

6. Using encouraging and affectionate words that express love and affection between family members, which we called

---

6   This blessed bread is called the Eulogia. These loaves are from the ones that were considered for the offering for Communion in the beginning of the Divine Liturgy. This is not the Communion body of Christ, but is a morsel dispensed to each person after the Liturgy.

"affective" communication, is very important for effective family communication. Be supportive and encourage each other. "Therefore comfort each other and edify one another, just as you also are doing" (1 Thess 5:11). Through encouragement, we build each other up. Encouragement can come through words or smiles. "I smiled on them when they had no confidence; and the light of my countenance they did not cast down" (Job 29:24, RSV). Job is speaking here about what he did in his life with his friends and others. When they were discouraged, he approved of them by his smile, and this encouraged them. His look of approval was precious to them and they appreciated it. We can encourage each other by smiles, by words, and by pointing out positives instead of negatives.

People who mine for gold find a lot of dirt in the process. They get rid of the dirt to find just a little piece of gold. They do not keep the dirt and dwell on it. They are looking for the gold. There is gold inside each one of us, but sometimes, when we dig into the other person's life or character, we dwell on the dirt and forget to search for the gold. It is better to throw the dirt away when you see it, until you get to the gold. Then, dwell on the gold. Try to see the positives in others, the gold, and do not try to hold on to the dirt, the iniquities in others.

Be positive. "A good report makes the bones healthy" (Prov 15:30). No one enjoys listening to negative comments or problems all the time. Be positive as much as possible, even when discussing a problem. Before presenting the problem, first discuss the positive aspects that exist regarding the issue. For example, before correcting your son's misbehavior, observe the positive qualities that he has and encourage him. Then, start talking about the negative point you want to correct.

This is what the Lord Jesus Christ did with the Samaritan woman. When He asked her to get her husband, she told Him that she did not have a husband. Before the Lord began speaking about her weakness, He told her, "You have well said, 'I have no husband'" (Jn 4:17). He complimented her. Then, He told her, "You have had five husbands, and the one whom you now have is not your husband" (Jn 4:18). Do you see His gentleness? He did not tell her that she is an adulteress living in sin. He was sensitive to her. Then, He ended with another compliment: "You spoke truly" (Jn 4:18). He told her about her weakness in between two compliments, and even then, He said it with such gentleness. That is why she went back to her town and told everyone, "Come, see a Man who told me all things that I ever did" (Jn 4:29). Imagine if the Lord had said, "You are an adulteress and an evil person. How could someone have five husbands and then live with a different man? Repent and change your life!" Do you think this woman would have told them, "Come, see a Man who told me all things that I ever did"? The Lord Jesus Christ's gentleness, positivity, and clear and direct communication encouraged and led this woman to repentance.

On the other hand, when you start with a negative statement, such as criticism or a complaint, you immediately make the other person defensive. Often, with our children, we use harsh words and tell them everything that is wrong with them. Very seldom do we tell them about the positive qualities in them. The children feel put down by their parents' negative remarks. Always start with positives. I am not saying that we should completely avoid discussing problems, conflicts, or issues, but when we discuss these serious issues, we need to do so in a positive way.

Couples who are dissatisfied with their relationships typically engage in more negative interaction than positive. The husband may always criticize his wife harshly. Perhaps she never hears a nice word from him. This is why sometimes spouses do not want to talk to each other; they are afraid of all the negativity. A happy person will not say many negative things. Therefore, if someone constantly criticizes his or her spouse, this may be a sign that he is not happy in his family life or in his marriage. He needs to find out why he is not happy and how to cure his unhappiness. Continuous criticism without discovering the reason for it complicates matters between spouses.

It is very important to learn how to compliment and encourage one another. When you say something positive, compliment, or encourage the other person, do not do this hypocritically. You need to be sincere and genuine. Mar Isaac the Syrian said, "Praise the other for his true positive qualities." If you are saying something positive and the other person feels that you are disingenuous, he may take it as a form of manipulation. For example, if someone is not usually positive with his wife and begins saying nice things, she may respond by saying, "Really! What is it that you want?"

7. Use "I" statements not "you" statements. "You" statements are a form of attack and make the other person defensive. The minute you say something like, "You are so selfish. How could you have done that?" the other person immediately thinks about how to defend himself. There is no need to attack. Some people attack others with a tone of self-righteousness, "I am more righteous than you," or "I am better than you," similar to the scribes and Pharisees. "Why does your Teacher eat with tax collectors and sinners?" (Mt 9:11). There is a tone of self-righteousness here. "Why do Your disciples transgress the tradition of the elders? For they do not wash their hands when they eat bread" (Mt 15:2). These statements are attacks resulting from the person's perception that he is more righteous than others. That is what we call a *judgmental* attitude. This is why it is better to avoid using statements beginning with "You," such as, "You never" or "You always."

Rather, "I" statements express how you feel. For example, instead of saying, "You neglect me," or "You hurt me," say, "I feel neglected." When you say, "I feel," what follows are your feelings and your feelings may be based on a correct perception or an incorrect one. However, when you say, "You neglect me," this is an accusation, and you make the other person defensive. He may not have meant to hurt or neglect you. Perhaps, you are a sensitive person. If you say, "I feel neglected," perhaps he will affirm his love to you and assure you that he does not mean to neglect you. In this way, matters will be resolved without attack.

38

8. When you talk about the other person, mention facts and not interpretations of the facts. There is a difference between saying, "You are late," "You forgot my birthday," or "You did not take me to this place like you said you would," which are facts, and saying, "You do not care about me," "You are an arrogant person," or "You only think about yourself; you are selfish." These are interpretations. It is better to mention facts, things that took place, and then, mention your feelings.

9. We tend to exaggerate, but that is not a good way to communicate. "I called you 20 times," and perhaps the phone only rang three times. Jacob said that Laban changed his wages ten times, which was an exaggeration (see Gen 31:7). In general, when someone exaggerates, the other finds a weak point and begins to argue: "It was only three times, not twenty times." In this way, the person who exaggerates discredits everything he says. This is similar to what happens with some newspapers or critics on the Internet; they exaggerate the information. People may listen to them once or twice, realize that they are untruthful, and stop reading that newspaper or listening to them. If they do read it, they would just read it for a laugh because they know it is all nonsense. They may also attack others harshly and even if what they say is true, the harshness causes the truth to be lost. Do not use exaggeration.

    Exaggeration is one way we vent our feelings when we are upset. If someone is upset with someone else, he may say, "You do this all the time!" This may relieve our inner tensions, but it does not promote marital harmony. Once your spouse feels any slight exaggeration on your part, he or she will feel fully justified in rejecting everything you have to say. Everything you say, whether valid or invalid, loses validity because of exaggeration. This is why words like "always" or "never" should be eliminated. His Holiness Pope Shenouda III of thrice blessed memory used to comment on this. When people sent him complaints containing phrases such as "*Everyone* in the church," His Holiness would respond, "Have you spoken to them one by one?"

10. Some people believe that they have the ability to read the minds and hearts of others. No matter how much you are able to understand other peoples' personalities or have an inclination about their thoughts or motives, you cannot say that you understand the other person with complete accuracy. When you are wrong, you can make the other person angry and ill at ease because you are reading him incorrectly. At the same time, you put the other person in a "no-win" situation. How can he defend himself or explain his point of view if you are convinced that you already understand? He will tell you that God is the only one who knows peoples' intentions. Mind reading is a very big obstacle in communication. If you assume that your estimation of our spouse's motives is completely accurate, you run the risk of provoking your spouse's temper. Therefore, to communicate effectively, do not attempt to read other peoples' minds nor pretend that you can.

11. It is not enough for you to express your feelings, but also explain what caused you to feel that way. If someone says, "I feel that you are ignoring me," this is a very general statement. You must explain what you mean by this and list the times when you felt ignored. Perhaps when you list the situations in which you felt ignored and the other person explains them to you, this will reveal that your perception was incorrect. Furthermore, sometimes we refuse to explain why we are upset. For example, if the husband is upset and his wife asks him why, he may say, "You should know why I am upset!" How would she know? "If you do not know on your own what is bothering me, what is the point of me telling you?" By saying this, he puts the other person in a no-win situation. This is not an effective way to communicate.

People often mistakenly assume that their feelings are universal; I assume that what upsets me upsets everyone else, so when I am upset, everybody should know I am upset. However, something may upset me, but it does not upset you, and something may upset you but not me. Therefore, we should not assume that people understand our feelings.

People may also simply retell what happened and let the story speak for itself, again expecting the other person to know what upset them. If you do not explain what is bothering you in the most specific language possible, your spouse will not understand. "When this happened, I felt this way, and this is what is bothering me."

12. Focus on preferences not principles. Principles deal with right and wrong. Many people confuse their preferences for principles and argue about whose opinion is right. As they argue, they desperately try to convince each other that they are right and in order to prove it, they may site statistics, books, and magazines and refer to examples of friends and neighbors. However, when you do this, you give the other person the chance to dispute your principle or the philosophy itself. On the other hand, if you say, "This is my preference," "my need," or "my wish," how can he dispute what you need? I will give you an example to clarify this point. If a wife expects her husband to help her with household chores and discusses this as a principle by stating that husbands should help their wives because now women work and help their husbands financially, etc., he can dispute it and they may argue with one another and never reach a resolution. However, if she discusses it as a preference, she may say, "I am really tired and exhausted when I get home, so if you help me, I will feel loved and appreciated." In this way, she is speaking about a preference, something she likes and that helps her. He cannot argue with her. Moreover, speaking about preferences opens the door to acceptance and makes it possible to reach a compromise.

Although we sometimes defend our preferences as principles and believe that we are making a strong argument, in reality, we weaken our argument. If you address these things as principles—matters of right and wrong—and each one is convinced that he is right, how can you compromise? Most likely you will clash. Most of these things are a matter of preference; one person prefers something while the other prefers something else. It would be much more productive if we talked about feelings and preferences, since this leaves room for compromise and resolution.

13. Communicate clearly and directly. You have to tell your spouse not only what bothers you, but also what you want done differently. This way, the other person will know what satisfies you. Some people have a very difficult time telling their spouses exactly what they want, and they insist that they should not have to ask. "He (or she) should know on his own what I want and if I have to ask, I would rather not have it." These people harbor the wish to have their needs fulfilled by their spouses without them being told. As we mentioned, it is difficult for us to express our needs. Of course, it would be very gratifying and nice to have your needs met without having to ask. However, it is not realistic to expect to have this kind of relationship all the time. God Himself tells us, "Until now you have asked nothing in My name. Ask, and you will receive, that your joy may be full" (Jn 16:24). He encourages us to ask.

I am often amazed about Adam. He was living in Paradise and had no stress whatsoever. He did not have a mortgage to pay, a job, bills, or exams. Nevertheless, he was upset. God brought him all the animals to name, and he found that each animal had one similar to it. However, he did not find someone comparable to him. God confirmed and validated his feelings. God did not belittle his feelings and say, "Why are you upset? Why do you always complain? You are living in paradise; what could possibly upset you?" On the contrary, God said, "It is not good that man should be alone; I will make him a helper comparable to him" (Gen 2:18). I want to emphasize here that God encourages us to ask, "Ask, and it will be given to you; seek, and you will find; knock, and it will be opened to you" (Mt 7:7).

Many people expect the other person to nurture them, like a mother with her child. A mother tries to meet all the needs of her baby without him asking, since babies cannot express themselves. However, spouses are not supposed to replicate this same level of care. God has instilled this level of nurture in the mother because children cannot ask, but we need to express our needs clearly.

14. Do not talk for a long time. Also, allow time for questions at the end. Some people have the ability to talk for hours without interruption, and without even needing to hear the other person's feedback. Do not give an hour-long lecture, leaving the other person frustrated and disengaged. You need to ensure that the other person is listening and following you. Talk and then ask for feedback. It is only through the questions of the listener that the speaker's words are fully understood. At the same time, pay attention to the listener's facial expressions. It is always a good idea to stop speaking before the other person loses patience. Perhaps his expressions reveal that he is upset, angry, or distracted. You can stop and ask, "What is your opinion about what I said?" This is to ensure that there is dialogue between you, and that it is not a monologue. Sometimes this occurs between parents and children. The child is not interested in listening to his father—he may be playing a game or sending a text message—but his father continues to lecture him and perhaps even starts yelling. You will not get your message across this way.

This also applies to confession or to talking with a priest. Do not keep repeating yourself; otherwise, the other person will get bored. I remember one time we were sitting with His Holiness Pope Shenouda III and someone was talking. He kept repeating himself over and over, so His Holiness looked at him kindly and said, "You should respect the intelligence of those who are listening to you." He meant, "We understand. Why do you keep repeating yourself?" A person may sometimes feel that there are many things he wants to say, pressing on him from within his heart, and he wants to say everything in his heart. However, this may result in losing the listener's attention.

15. Limit yourself to one or two topics per conversation.

Sometimes, if a wife has been trying to have a discussion with her husband who is avoidant, she might accumulate many things she wants to discuss. When he finally agrees to talk, she brings up twenty or thirty points. Of course, this urge is understandable, especially if the other spouse is avoidant, but it is unhealthy because it will overwhelm the discussion. It could also be counterproductive because the listener will start to lose patience, and at the same time the speaker will not be able to speak deeply or explore the issues in depth. Thank God that he sat to talk with you and is listening, and tries to focus on one or two issues at most. In my opinion, if you resolve one or two, these will influence five or six other issues indirectly. There is no issue that just "hangs" by itself. If you look at all the issues, you will find that they are connected to each other.

Relationships begin and develop through communication. We cannot sustain a relationship without communication. Communication is what we do to give and get understanding. The quality of communication has a direct impact on the quality of the relationship. When we have effective communication, we are satisfied in our relationships. Effective communication is the cornerstone of strong, healthy relationships. Effective communication occurs when the message sent is the same message that is received. This point is very important. Problems arise when messages on either end are misunderstood. In other words, problems may occur if there is misunderstanding or miscommunication.

Communicating with God

Why are there so many denominations, although we use the same Bible? The problem is in the interpretation—private interpretation. People interpret verses in the way that makes them comfortable. Which interpretation is accurate? The Orthodox one, the Catholic one, or the Protestant one? Why should I say that my interpretation is correct and theirs is not? If I wrote a letter and sent it to ten people, and the ten people read it, which one of them can I say understood it correctly? The one who understood it correctly is the one who was able to discover the meaning that was in *my* mind when I wrote it. When the message sent by God and the message received by me is the same, this is the true interpretation.

If someone says, "This is what this verse means to me," with all due respect, who cares about your personal private interpretation? I care about what *God* means by this verse. It is not difficult to discover God's meaning because "God is not the author of confusion" (1 Cor 14:33). He does not want to confuse us. God's message is direct and clear. However, sometimes we do not feel comfortable with God's message, so we twist it in order to meet our desires and make ourselves comfortable. Therefore, when we study and interpret the Holy Bible, the challenge is to discover the meaning intended by God for this message. This would be the accurate and true interpretation of the Holy Bible. You discover this by using internal validity, i.e., comparing one verse with others inside the text, and also by external practice, meaning how the Church understood and applied this verse throughout the ages. By using both together, comparing history with the context and comparison with other verses that discuss the same topic, you will be able to discover the meaning intended by God, even if it makes you uncomfortable.

Feeling uncomfortable is actually what causes someone to change. For example, if they turned up the air conditioning right now and the room became very cold, we would feel uncomfortable and leave. Thus, what catalyzes change *is* feeling uncomfortable. The word of God sometimes makes us uncomfortable so that we can change our former and sinful behavior and walk according to His commandments. When the Holy Bible says that the people were "cut to the heart" (Acts 2:37), this means that the word of God pierced their souls.

In order to have effective communication between us and God, the message sent by God needs to be the same message received by us. This is the accurate interpretation. This is a very important point regarding the Holy Bible.

Communication in the Service

We may not realize the importance of effective communication, but it is *very* important. It is even important in the service. I was recently asked about the most important quality I look for when choosing a priest. In addition to the general conditions, such as spirituality, education, biblical knowledge, etc., I observe his ability to communicate effectively. Why? A priest deals with all sorts of people, old and young, rich and poor, educated and illiterate, people who grew up here and people who grew up in Egypt, and people that come from other churches, such as Eritrean or Ethiopian. If he does not know how to communicate effectively with each person, it would be very difficult to interact with such a vast array of people. You may find a spiritual person who has biblical knowledge, but cannot communicate well with everyone. He may only be able to communicate with a certain group of people. For example, he is successful in serving the youth, but he has nothing to do with other people. Or, someone knows how to deal with adults very well, but does not know how to communicate with children or youth. This could be a weak point. Another person may attend a church and clash with everyone—the church board members, the service coordinator, and the deacons; in a very short period of time, you would find numerous problems. He is not familiar with how to communicate effectively.

Therefore, effective communication is important in the service, in the family, and in relationships. It is also important in our relationships with civil authorities. Whenever there is good communication, there is opportunity for success. Poor communication leads to failure. Thus, a very important trait in every Christian person who is a child of God is the ability to communicate well with each person. The Lord Jesus Christ was able to communicate with the poor and the rich, the sinners and the righteous, the adults and the children. When the disciples wanted to send the children away, He said, "Let the little children come to Me, and do not forbid them; for of such is the kingdom of heaven" (Mt 19:14). Without effective communication with God first, we will be unable to communicate effectively with others. May the Lord provide us with the ability to communicate effectively with others for the glory of His name.

3 Barriers to Communication

Being too Busy

Inappropriate Atmosphere

Choice of Words

Sarcasm, Criticism, and Blaming Others

Lack of Confidentiality

Ignoring the Other Person

Inability to Talk as Friends

Conflict

Communicating our thoughts and feelings with kindness and understanding is essential for a healthy family life. This is called "affective" communication. The word *affective* comes from the word *affection*, which refers to emotions and feelings. Unfortunately, many of us do not learn communication skills and instead of communicating well, we often build barriers and walls. (Communication skills are learned in the home. As parents, you are supposed to teach your children, from an early age, how to communicate well.) As we identify the barriers that hinder communication between family members, and as we learn to love as the Lord Jesus Christ taught us, we will learn how to build bridges. If we already have barriers, learning how to build bridges will improve our communication within the family, which will eventually lead to love and understanding. There are many barriers to communication; below I identify eight important ones.

Being too Busy

We do not have enough time to spend quality time together or to discuss our concerns and issues. There are many activities and demands that compete for our time, including work, household chores, television, Internet, sports, social relationships, church service, etc. Parents often become involved in the tasks of daily life and are unwilling to stop what they are doing to listen to their children. When we do not listen to them and validate their opinions, they are more likely to look outside the home for someone to listen to them. When your child asks to spend time with you or play with you, this is a great chance to build a strong bond between you. However, if you are too busy, you will miss this opportunity to build a loving relationship. If the message we are sending to our children is, "Go away, and do not bother me right now," they will gradually withdraw themselves from our lives. Later, when they are teenagers, we will beg them to spend time with us and wonder why they are so distant.

Good communication leads to good relationships. However, communication, the core of our relationships, sometimes takes a backseat to the many other activities. We do not just sit down and share our thoughts and feelings with each other. The surprising thing is that when couples are engaged, they have plenty of time to discuss things with each other. Why does this change after marriage? Are couples less busy during the engagement period, or was communication between them a high priority during that time? I believe it is the fact that communication was a high priority at that time. Saying, "I am too busy" is just an excuse we use. If you are a believer in good communication and in the time that you spend together, you will find the time to make it happen, with your spouse or your children. "When there is a will, there is a way." If you make this a priority, you will find the time for it. If you do not, you will find that other responsibilities take up most of your time. This is why we need to set aside time for conversations and enriching our relationships, as spouses and as parents and children. We have to designate time for our family when we plan our schedules.

The problem that all of us face is that when there is less time, there is much less quality time. A marriage or relationship cannot be strong and healthy if we are not doing anything to make it better. Without time for communication, we easily end up like the lonely man in Ecclesiastes 4:8–12. In this passage, King Solomon describes a lonely man who has a lot of money and many things to do, but no one to talk to. "There is one alone, without companion: He has neither son nor brother. Yet there is no end to all his labors, nor is his eye satisfied with riches. But he never asks, 'For whom do I toil and deprive myself of good?' This also is vanity and a grave misfortune" (Eccl 4:8). What is the benefit if you are very busy and wealthy, but you have no friends or are not friends with your spouse? Solomon calls this "a grave misfortune."

We have to understand that quality time together does not just happen; you need to plan for it. When we sit together one-on-one, this creates a bond between the family members, which becomes stronger with each experience. This bond grows deeper each time parents sit together as a couple or sit and talk with their children. During that time, the children begin feeling secure and comfortable. Only then will they drop their defenses and let down their guard. They will start opening up to their parents and sharing their secrets, thoughts, questions, feelings, and weaknesses.

How can I make a bridge to overcome this specific barrier? Set aside a regular block of time to deal with issues, and a different block of time to enjoy your family's company. Set aside time for "instrumental" communication, since sometimes there are issues encountered by couples which require designated time for discussion. Set another time for "affective" communication. Do not combine the two. You will be surprised how powerful it can be for the two of you to simply agree to set time aside to enjoy each other's company as friends, without dealing with conflicts or issues. I have noticed that the majority of families in the United States seem to fight the most during vacations and holidays. We have to draw the line between time for friendship and time for discussing issues.

[For more on this, please refer to Chapter 3 and Chapter 5]

Inappropriate Atmosphere

It is very important to avoid an inappropriate atmosphere. Atmosphere can be inappropriate with regards to time or place. For example, it is not right to try to discuss an important issue while getting ready for work or for church early in the morning. Both the husband and wife are stressed and tense because there is not much time, so they end up fighting without resolving the problem. Communication is always difficult when the atmosphere is wrong. If the other person is tired, hungry, angry, busy, or involved with friends, it is not right to discuss your issues right then and there. It is also harder to communicate when we are surrounded by distractions that interrupt our conversation. When we try to communicate in such an environment, we usually feel impatient or very angry, and we just want to rush through the conversation. The spirit of cooperation cannot exist when feelings of impatience or anger rule, and the result is often confusion and hurt feelings.

We have to carefully choose the place and time to be able to have effective conversations. This is why we need to set aside times when we are calm and receptive to the Spirit. Being "receptive to the Spirit" means being connected with the Holy Spirit and being able to talk to each other by God's grace. "Let no corrupt word proceed out of your mouth, but what is good for necessary edification, that it may impart grace to the hearers" (Eph 4:29). The location, setting, or circumstances should be comfortable, private, and conducive to conversation. If there is an issue between the couple, they should not discuss it in front of their children. Otherwise, the children will be involved in everything and aware of everything. That is not right. Privacy is essential.

When the atmosphere is right, we must be willing to focus on the other person and give them our undivided attention. This shows respect and makes the other person feel validated, important, and appreciated. In this type of atmosphere, we are more willing to listen, respond kindly, and solve problems constructively.

Choice of Words

Words are very powerful. You can change someone by merely using words. The words we use to express our thoughts or feelings can present one of the biggest barriers to effective communication. Sometimes, the words we use can have two possible meanings, and this can cause a lot of confusion and misunderstanding. The words we use can sometimes convey a different meaning to the listener than they do to us. For example, if the spouses are from two different cultures, such as Egyptian and Syrian, their dialects differ, and one word may mean two different things. If a word is misunderstood in the correct context, this can cause problems.

Other times, we incorrectly assume that the person with whom we are talking will understand certain terms we are using. This mainly occurs between parents and children. Parents may assume that their children know the meanings of certain words that they actually have not yet learned. They may yell at their children or punish them for not doing what was asked of them without realizing that the children did not understand what was asked. This is why you have to make sure that your children fully understand what you say to them. We cannot communicate with others when we express words or ideas they may not understand. Clarification is important.

In order to bridge this barrier, the message needs to be clear in your mind before speaking to the other person. It is good to organize your thoughts and choose the appropriate words before starting to speak. We must also use language that matches the experience and level of understanding of the listener. Many misunderstandings could be avoided if we ask in quiet sincerity, "Do you see what I am trying to say?" We could ask them to paraphrase what was said to make sure they understood it correctly. At the same time, if you are the listener, you could ask, "Is this what you mean?" This kind of feedback can correct misunderstandings and help spouses or children clarify their own feelings.

Sarcasm, Criticism, and Blaming Others

Sometimes, people make fun of others, then claim that they were just joking and did not mean anything by it. Other people may be harshly critical or constantly blame others. "There is one who speaks like the piercings of a sword, but the tongue of the wise promotes health" (Prov 12:18). Sarcasm can cause more pain than a sword. Speech that resembles the piercings of a sword can completely destroy family relationships.

When you trust the other person and feel safe, you begin sharing personal weaknesses or vulnerable information with each other. For example, imagine a moment of love and friendship between the spouses in which one of them felt that he could completely pour out his heart to the other person. He opened his heart and talked about an incident that happened to him, perhaps in childhood or at work. At the time, the other person listened, showed love and understanding, and was supportive. A few months later, they have a fight. The other person then takes the incident that was mentioned before and uses it against her spouse. She may say, "Everybody says this about you! Remember the story you told me about your childhood?" The information that was shared in a time of love was used as a dagger or a sword to pierce the other person. Do you think that this person will be ready to open his heart and share things like this again? It would be very difficult. No one is going to continue sharing personal and vulnerable information if it might be used against him later.

After Adam and Eve ate from the tree, they covered themselves with fig leaves as a method of self-defense. They covered up their differences because they were afraid of being rejected by the other.

Similarly, some people stop sharing things with their spouses because whenever they do, they do not receive support. Whenever a person does not find love or acceptance in the other person, he begins to cover up his differences and hide behind the fig leaves. He no longer wants to uncover himself in front of the other person because he is afraid of rejection.

Having a sarcastic, critical, judgmental, whiny, accusatory, or demanding attitude destroys good relationships. No one wants to be criticized, placed on the defensive, or misjudged all the time. When you develop this attitude, you attack the person, not the problem. The person is not your enemy; rather, the problem is your enemy. Attacking the problem, or trying to solve it, should be our goal. Sometimes, when children make mistakes or do not perform as we believe they should, we overreact, accuse, and attack them. Our reactions are not proportional to their mistakes. This kind of message communicates to our children that they are worthless and that it is impossible for them to change. For example, continually telling younger children that they will go to Hell or that God is going to hate them for doing this or that will cause them to think, "Why should I try if I am already going to hell?" The child will believe that this is his fate, since that is the message he is receiving. Instead of telling him that God will hate him and send him to hell if he lies, we can tell him God loves him no matter what, but telling the truth is pleasing to God. It is the same message, but said in a positive way.

When we avoid interrupting, criticizing, or judging, and when we focus on problems and solutions instead of attacking the individual, family members will feel free to express ideas and feelings without fear of blame or rejection. When we communicate kindly, lovingly, and affectionately, others will feel safe and secure to share their feelings without fear. With confession fathers, sometimes a young person will mention one of his sins while looking at the priest's reaction. If the priest overreacts and becomes tense, the person will be less willing to share the rest of his sins. This also happens to parents. The child may narrate the beginning of a story to see how you react to it. If you get angry or he feels that he is being blamed, he will immediate hide the rest of the story. They will discuss their problems openly if they know they will not be lectured or scolded.

One reason for this barrier is having an unforgiving spirit. This can cause someone to constantly blame others, criticize others, or become sarcastic. We have to forgive one another regarding mistakes made in the past, so that the trust upon which the friendship flourishes can be nurtured. Another reason for blame and criticism is feeling inferior to others. This happens a lot between spouses if, for example, a wife makes more money than her husband or has a higher position than him at the same company. The husband may feel insecure and feel inferior to her. In these cases, he always criticizes her, blames her, and puts her down. He would have to work on this by building and improving his self-confidence. Then, he would cease projecting his insecurities onto his wife. We have to realize that we are not at the mercy of our issues. We should not constantly blame or criticize others just because of bad experiences we have had in the past. You should be in control of your issues, and not let them control you.

Lack of Confidentiality

We need to train ourselves, as a family, to understand that family matters should be kept within the family. A girl heard her friends at church relating details of a private conversation she had shared with her mother two days earlier. Her mom had told her friend's mother, who then told her friend, who told other friends, etc. This daughter will never share anything with her mother again. Our children must know that we do not reveal their secrets without their permission. Family members need to know that there is certain information that is ours alone and will not be shared. This can even include happy secrets, and the family can agree to keep them to themselves for a certain period of time. For example, if the wife becomes pregnant, they can decide when they will share this information with others. In this way, you are training the entire family to value confidentiality. Keeping some secrets together as a family tells your child that you will keep other information confidential also. Lack of confidentiality can inhibit free exchange between family members.

Trust is essential for good communication. If I know that when I tell you something, you will not share it with anyone else, I will be encouraged to share more information. Sometimes, we reveal a secret to others, thinking that it will go no further, but then it gets passed from one person to the next, with each person telling the next, "Do not tell anyone!" A family once complained to me about a priest because he had not visited them during a certain period of time when they were in need. However, that priest had actually been sick and in the hospital during that time. They were extremely upset with Abouna; thus, I told them that he had been hospitalized so they could understand the reason and let it go. I also told them that it was confidential information and that I did not want anyone to know; they assured me that they would tell no one. The next morning, I got a phone call from a member of the congregation asking me, "We heard that Abouna had a heart attack!" This is a funny story, yet it shows how information spreads and changes because everyone adds his or her own small details. The entire church became aware that Abouna had been in the hospital, and I was the one who had released the information.

What if you are a mother and after your daughter tells you something, she says, "Do not tell Dad"? What should you do? From their childhood, you have to always tell your children, "You need to trust that I will use the information that you will tell me for your best interest. Do you not you trust your mother? Be sure that I will use it for your best interest." In this way, you are not promising them something you will later fail to uphold, and you gain their trust. If you promise them something, you should not break your promise. Thus, in this way, you did not bind yourself by a promise, and at the same time, if you felt that this information should be shared with the other parent, you will share it.

Trust is essential to good communication and we build trust by maintaining confidence. Family matters should be kept within the family. Our children must know that we do not reveal their secrets without their permission. I do not like it when parents go into their children's rooms to look for things or go through their email without their permission, etc. It is very important to keep an eye on your child. Be aware of what he is doing, but do not do anything behind his back or invade his privacy without his permission. That is not right.

Ignoring the Other Person

When a parent ignores a child, or an older child ignores a younger sibling, communication breaks down. Sometimes, we ignore messages because we think we already know what is being said. We do not want to hear the message, or we are too busy thinking of our response. Sometimes, we do not respect the speaker and, therefore, do not listen to him. Children who are ignored turn to someone else, often someone outside the family, who will listen to them. If you ignore your children, they will find more than one friend who is willing to listen to them. In this way, you build a wall between you and your children.

We need to respect others. When we respect others, we listen to them and do not ignore them. As we listen to our children, they will feel our respect for them. They will know that we accept and respect their opinions. Each family member, even young children, can be asked to contribute ideas and opinions at family meetings or discussions. Sometimes, young children feel ignored in family conversations; thus, you should ask them, "What do you think about this?" Include their feelings and responses, whatever they are, to reach a solution. Show them that you respect their opinions and value what they think and feel. This makes them feel validated, loved, and respected. Such responses as, "I am glad you brought up this idea," or "That is a good observation" can also show your appreciation for your child's ideas and suggestions.

We can teach them that they are part of the decision-making process, and how to think correctly and make good choices. When we show them that we value their judgment, they will feel that they have something worthwhile to share. This increases their sense of belonging in the family. Unfortunately, many of our children just want to turn eighteen so they can move out of the house because they do not feel they belong to the family. That is not good. However, if they feel that they contribute to their family with their opinions and that their opinions are respected, welcomed, and valued, they will have a sense of belonging and will not feel undervalued.

Inability to Talk as Friends

Another barrier is the inability to talk as friends. Tension and conflict are pervasive when the spouses talk to one another. No one wants to live in an argumentative environment all the time. Some people prefer to withdraw themselves from conversations in order to avoid an argument. Many spouses were friends at the beginning, but the friendship ended. Where did the friendship go? The strongest marriages are those in which the couple maintains a solid friendship over the years. Couples should maintain a deep respect for one another as friends who are able to share everything in an atmosphere of deep acceptance.

If someone constantly brings up issues that make you tense, you will choose not to talk to that person in the future. Think for a moment about a friendship that you enjoy with someone other than your spouse, a friend whom you love and with whom you enjoy spending time, someone to whom you go whenever you feel stressed or overwhelmed. Think about what you discuss with that friend when you are together. How often do you have to talk to that person about problems between the two of you? Friends are not people with whom we argue a lot. Of course, from time to time we may disagree, but most of the time, we enjoy our time together and find comfort.

Friends discuss common interests, things both of them enjoy and that make both of them happy. If you both love soccer, you talk about soccer. If you love politics, you talk about politics. Two deacons who love hymns may discuss hymns. Sometimes, you just simply talk. Friends can talk about spiritual matters, politics, philosophy of life, sports, fun things they have done, or dreams about the future. On the other hand, some couples just have conversations about problems— problems with their children, finances, work, in-laws, etc. There is a major difference here. Discussing issues and problems all the time can easily cause communication to break down. If all our conversations revolve around problems or the concerns of life, and we lose our ability to talk as friends, this will completely suffocate the feelings of friendship and warmth between the spouses. If couples are not careful, most of their conversations end up around problems and concerns, not points of view or points of interest. The question here is, do you talk as friends, or not? If all your discussions are about problems and concerns, you do not talk as friends.

While it is important to discuss problems and concerns, there should be a specific time for this, which should be completely separate from the time for friendship. You need to set aside time to discuss problems, and both of you need to be emotionally prepared for the discussion. If you are not talking about problems, it is time for friendship and you should talk about things that you enjoy doing together. If you think about a problem or concern that needs to be discussed, it requires self-discipline in order to postpone talking about the issue until the proper time—the time that you allotted to discuss problems.

To talk as friends, you need to also listen as friends. Good friends listen with minimal defensiveness. When you share with a friend, you do not worry about whether your friend's feelings are getting hurt or whether he is offended. You know that you are in a safe atmosphere. This is because a friend is someone who is glad to see you and does not have any immediate plans for your improvement. Spouses, on the other hand, usually want to change and improve each other. Therefore, when talking as friends, you are not trying to change one another; you can both relax and enjoy the conversation. When we lose this ability to talk as friends, we become less interested in communicating because our conversations are no longer enjoyable.

How many hours a week should we designate for friendship and how many hours for discussing problems? It would be nice to agree that *all* the time will be for friendship and affective communication, and that you will only discuss issues during the time allotted for them. This will enrich the relationship. The default is friendship; you should be treating each other as friends all the time. The *exception* is the time you spend discussing issues. If the spirit of true love and friendship existed between a couple all the time, there would be a strong bond connecting them. In them, the words of the Holy Bible would be fulfilled, "They are no longer two but one" (Mt 19:6). To truly live in love and friendship, you should train yourselves to always enjoy one another's company. Even when you discuss these issues, it should be done in the spirit of true friendship, love, and understanding.

If it happens that you are enjoying your friendship time and a conflict is about to surface, you have to pay attention to this in order to avoid ruining your quality time. We need to say, "This is not the time for conflicts or issues." Otherwise, the devil will always try to ruin our quality time by bringing up a conflict to weaken the relationship among the family members. For example, a husband may take his wife out to a nice restaurant in order to enjoy one another's company. They order the food and start talking. One of them brings up a problem or something that happened with the children that day. Then, the good time they were supposed to have turns upside down; he gets angry, she gets upset, the meal is not enjoyed, and they go home frustrated. The purpose of the outing was mainly to enjoy each other's company, but it became a source of misery and sadness. We can be in control of this time and train ourselves to talk as friends. Therefore, if you set aside time to talk as friends, do not be tempted to discuss any problems during that time because these issues may ruin your time together. Keep your focus on friendship. If your focus is on conflict or differences, you will lose your focus on one another. Even with relationship issues, there is too much temptation to solve the problem and give advice. Let this time be to focus on one another, on one another's needs, and not on conflict.

[For more on how to talk as friends, please refer to Chapter 5.]

Conflict

The last barrier is conflict. When people argue, they usually get upset and stop talking altogether. Conflict is a major barrier to communication. Communication may get disrupted when issues arise in the relationship. The couple may be having a relaxing, friendly conversation, when suddenly it intensifies for some reason, until it reaches the point that they stop talking to one another. That is why it is very important to learn how to manage conflict. If conflict is not managed well, the increasing perception becomes that talking leads to fighting. If this happens, it can cause the couple to avoid any conversations in order to avoid arguments, which is the worst possible outcome.

If a disagreement or a misunderstanding occurs between you,

do not focus on trying to solve the problem immediately. You may need more information in order to better understand the issue. Quick fixes sometimes complicate things. Friends do not focus on solving problems or giving unwanted advice; they listen more than anything else. A wife may tell her husband about a problem she has at work. She already knows what she will do to take care of it, but she tells her husband because she needs support and somebody to listen to her, not because she needs a solution. If her husband starts yelling at her and saying things like, "This happened because you did not listen. That is the way you are! This is what you have to do…" she will learn not to tell him next time. She would choose to save herself a lecture and not share things with him, since he gives her unwanted advice and does not listen. He is not empathetic nor supportive of her decisions.

Your advice as a husband will be valued much more if she asks for it. Do not just volunteer it because, most likely, she does not need it. Your advice may be very valuable, but if it is given at the wrong time, it will be ignored. This happens with us as fathers of confession. Many people come to us just because they need someone to listen to them, but we sometimes give too much advice too quickly and offend the listener. When you are pressed to solve a problem, it is easy to cut off discussions that can bring you closer together as a couple.

In conclusion, recognizing the barriers to communication and understanding how they can be overcome will help us express the love we feel within our families. When communication is used as a vehicle for expressing love, it becomes a powerful force in uniting and strengthening families. Good communication leads to good relationships.

Part II
NECESSARY VIRTUES FOR HEALTHY RELATIONSHIPS

---

4 Trust in the Family

Trust and Mistrust
    Trust between Parents and Children
    Trust between Spouses

Primary and Secondary Trust
    Secondary Trust
    Primary Trust

Intimacy

Trust in Marriage
    Intimacy in Body
    Untimacy of Mind
    Intimacy of Spirit

Rebuilding Trust
    Honesty
    Congruence
    Avoid Scorekeeping
    Accountability
    Time

Trust and Mistrust

Pain is both good and bad. It is bad in itself because it is a sign of suffering, but it is good in that it indicates that something is wrong; therefore, it protects you. In the same way, although mistrust is bad, it is good in that it protects you. You will not completely trust someone while you are still getting to know him. You will be reserved at the beginning and trust will be built gradually. In general, trust should be earned and not given.

Mistrust is an instinct that God instilled in us, one that is absolutely necessary in order to survive. Without it, we may be exposed to dangerous or hurtful situations. As a result, we are prone to be reserved when meeting someone new. As the relationship grows, we learn to trust and continue to trust unless damaging events occur. I believe this is no less true in the parent/child relationship. We trust our children to abide by the rules of safety and conduct that we have laid out for them. However, sometimes events can occur to damage this trust between parents and children. At this point, the children must earn trust.

<u>Trust between Parents and Children</u>

Trust in the parent/child relationship is often a controversial topic. For parents in search of guidance, many parenting books recommend absolute trust and say that parents should completely trust their children. The authors argue that children need the assurance that their parents trust in their abilities. This need for trust in the relationship is certainly true. However, if we just make a blanket statement that "parents should give absolute trust to their children all the time," this can be very dangerous. I hope that the professionals writing these books are assuming that the child has not been coming home drunk or slipping out of the house at night, or that the child has never been arrested or acted violently or in an abusive manner. In all of these situations, parents should be concerned, and children should need to earn the trust of their parents.

Unfortunately, many parents take the advice of absolute trust as a given without the logical "if / then" qualifiers. It is because they love their children that they put qualifiers on trust. There is no contradiction between this and unconditional love. God loves us unconditionally, so much so that He cannot leave us to lead a sinful life. Thus, these qualifiers do not negate unconditional love.

Can a child earn trust again after such events as we mentioned above? The answer is yes, he can absolutely earn trust again. He has to earn it, and he should feel proud and empowered that he earned it back. Thus, the theory of earned trust is a purely instinctive sense. Trust should be earned, not given. Just because we are parents and love our children, this is not reason enough to trust them when their behaviors deem otherwise.

Trust between Spouses

The same can apply to trust between spouses. Is trust or a lack thereof affecting your marital relationship? The issue of trust often comes up when counseling spouses. I want you to consider that your spouse may have been burned in another relationship. For example, maybe he had a relationship before getting married, and he was hurt by the other person's behavior in that relationship. This caused him to enter into marriage with damaged or broken trust, which can be reflected in the current situation. Has infidelity or something else in your relationship made it hard for you and your spouse to trust each other? If so, you are not alone. Many spouses suffer from mistrust amongst themselves.

When couples are asked to describe a situation that causes distress in their relationship, the topic of trust frequently arises. For example,

- "I cannot trust him with the checkbook!"

- "She never gets home when she says she will!"

- "He always says, 'Trust me, I will get it done,' but he never does."

- "I do not trust her around other men. She is always flirting."

These comments indicate the presence of a low level of trust in the relationship. Although trust between spouses clearly leads to a feeling of safety and connectedness, many couples do not know how to develop or maintain a trusting relationship. At the end, I will give you five ingredients to help you earn one another's trust.

Many spouses expect trust to be automatically granted as a component of commitment. This is not right because trust should be earned; it is not given automatically. However, they feel that they deserve to be trusted without putting forth any effort to foster trust. Another problem with trust is that some people believe that once trust is lost, it can never be regained. I want to emphasize that trust should be earned, and if it is lost, it *can* be earned again. What these couples do not realize is that with the right ingredients, trust can be built, strengthened, and maintained regardless of the past. Thus, mutual love and respect can be intentionally and purposefully increased.

Primary and Secondary Trust

From the time a person is born until he dies, trust is the foundation of all healthy relationships, such as relations between baby and mother, husband and wife, business manager and employee, or terminally ill patient and caregiver. The final element of trust occurs in two forms: Primary Trust and Secondary Trust. According to Merriam Webster online dictionary, the definition of trust is: "Assured reliance on (or confidence in) the character, ability, strength, or truth of someone or something." This is secondary trust. The Holy Bible tells us that trust is being confident that you are secure; this is primary trust. Note the difference between the two. Secondary trust is confidence in the other person, in his honesty, integrity, ability, and character. Primary trust, as the Holy Bible says, means that a person is secure: "Behold, God is my salvation, I will trust and not be afraid" (Is 12:2). I am secure because God is my salvation; therefore, I will trust Him and I will not be afraid. "The Lord, is my strength and song; He also has become my salvation" (Is 12:2). That is why there is no contradiction between Webster's definition and the definition in Isaiah 12:2. Webster gives us the accurate definition of secondary trust, while Isaiah describes abiding primary trust, i.e., feeling secure and safe in the world around you.

God's original design for us is to have intimacy with Him. The main reason we feel secure in the world is because God is our salvation. This feeling of being secure in the world through our intimate relationship with God will help us build secondary trust, which is intimacy with others. When both forms of trust are solidly rooted in our lives, we can maintain stability and sanity even in times of personal crisis and trouble. In other words, together, primary and secondary trust help us cope correctly with crises. That is why I would like to discuss primary and secondary trust in more detail.

<u>Secondary Trust</u>

Let us start with secondary trust, or trusting others. In day-to-day relationships, secondary trust is established by the other person and is based on what he or she does or does not do. It is based on the other person, and not on me; it is earned. That is why we say that secondary trust is like the stock market: When the other person performs well, trust goes up. When he or she performs poorly, trust goes down. For example, I may agree to loan my friend my laptop because previous experiences revealed that he was responsible and dependable. He earned my trust and that is why I can give him my laptop without hesitation. Previous experience may have begun with less expensive tools, because no one ever lends something very expensive at the beginning. I start by lending less expensive things and, gradually, trust is built. The more I trust him, the more I can risk more expensive things. As long as he maintains his good track record, I trust him.

Our trust gets tested in proportion to the value we place on the item someone is borrowing. The higher the value, the more trust is needed. When a relationship is new, we may risk loaning something that is easily repaired or replaced. We will not risk something very valuable in the beginning. If an item has very strong sentimental value, we weigh the value of the item against the value of the relationship. As risk increases, more trust is required. Therefore, what happens if the stakes are even higher, such as sharing our heart with someone else? This is something extremely valuable, so it needs more trust.

Such a request might seem too risky or almost unthinkable if we have previously suffered a broken heart or not learned how to trust while growing up. If people did not develop secondary trust due to previous experiences or relationships, such as with parents or family members, they will most likely enter into marriage with mistrust. How can they trust to give and share their hearts and their love with someone else when they do not have trust in their hearts? For example, consider if a person's needs were not met during childhood, or if his parents ignored his feelings of rejection, shame, or frustration. These types of encounters during the formative years actually set in place a type of trust template, which is mistrust, and this will affect his entire life, especially marital life. That is why, as parents, you need to deal with these issues in order for your children to develop trust. Thus, when they enter into marriage, they can start on the right foundation. People like this are ill equipped for establishing healthy and trusting relationships. Unless their wounds are acknowledged and healed, their vulnerability may lead to destructive habits. they will tend to be more vulnerable to addiction, or they may enter into relationships with people who are addicts.

Primary Trust

Primary trust is feeling safe and secure, and it begins in the mother's womb while the person is still an embryo. While most people are familiar with secondary trust, primary trust is actually more critical to the healthy development of the inner person. Primary trust helps you develop your character, and is referred to as the *intrapersonal* relationship. Secondary trust is interpersonal, i.e., between you and others. Primary trust is the foundation upon which secondary trust is built. If we have security in our hearts, interpersonal relationships will be easy.

Most specialists agree that the first 18 months of a child's life set the stage for establishing a personal sense of primary trust. However, few realize that even the months before a child is born, while he is in his mother's uterus, are also critical to the development of primary trust. For generations, women have encouraged pregnant mothers to think good thoughts and listen to cheerful music in order to have healthy, happy babies. These things have been passed down from grandmothers to mothers to daughters, but they do not know why. In fact, these things help a child develop trust. People across the globe have passed this message along to their children and grandchildren. However, some people think that this information is superstitious and downplay this advice.

There are verses in the Holy Bible that talk about trust beginning in the womb. "But You are He who took Me out of the womb; You made Me trust while on My mother's breasts" (Ps 22:9). The infant started trusting in God when he was in his mother's womb. Also, God told Jeremiah, "Before I formed you in the womb I knew you" (Jer 1:5). This shows the intimate relationship with God. As I mentioned, primary trust comes from our relationship with God; this is our security, since we are His children. In the Gospel account according to St. Luke, Elizabeth said to St. Mary, "As soon as the voice of your greeting sounded in my ears, the babe leaped in my womb for joy" (Lk 1:44). He leaped for joy because he felt secure and happy; that is primary trust. In Psalm 139, David says that God knew him while he was still being formed in the womb (see verses 15 and 16). David further proclaims, in the same Psalm, that he put his trust in God from that time. Thus, trust begins while we are in our mother's womb.

Newborn babies do not yet have the cognitive function to rationally place their trust in another (secondary trust). They have not yet developed this function of how to evaluate others so they can trust them. However, they use their instincts in order to know whether or not the world around them is safe and secure.

Some medical research has interestingly verified the concept of primary trust.[7] One study revealed that preborn babies tighten into fetal curves when their mothers smoke a cigarette. They feel that it is unsafe and dangerous to them, and that is why they tighten into fetal curves. Not only this, but the baby also feels pain from the cigarette toxins coming through the umbilical cord, and that is why he acts in this way. In fact, it was scientifically proven that a baby tightens his abdominal muscles when his mother even *thinks* about smoking a cigarette. This shows that there is a mysterious bond between the mother and child, which we are trying to understand from a scientific point of view. However, it is clear that a person's sense of trust can begin to develop and can be harmed very early in life, even when he

---

7   https://www.ncbi.nlm.nih.gov/pmc/articles/PMC3581096/

is still an embryo in his mother's womb.

Of course, if it starts in the mother's womb, it will continue outside the womb. The first few years of a child's life are essential to building primary trust, especially the first 18 months. After a child is born, primary trust will either be strengthened or weakened depending on early childhood experiences, including how parents deal with the child. A child's perspective about himself and about life is based on what happens at home. Primary trust is lost or weakened in children who are brought up in families in which the parents fight or yell and scream at each other frequently, or in which the word "divorce" is frequently mentioned.

When love, stability, safety, and forgiveness are balanced with fair and proper discipline, a child learns that he is valued and appreciated regardless of his performance. Please note that balance is required between love and forgiveness, and fair and proper discipline.

Furthermore, a child's perspective about God will be built on his perception of his parents. When we pray, we say, "Our Father who art in heaven." Thus, we usually form an image in our minds about God, our Father, based on our relationship with our parents. For example, if my parents are controlling, I may perceive God as controlling. If my parents are permissive, I may perceive God as permissive. Since a child still cannot enter into a direct relationship with God, he forms the image of Him in his mind from the image of his parents. That is why the way parents deal with their children in the first years of their childhood is not only important in building primary trust, but also in building the right image of God. A child's perspective of God is formed in the early years and is based largely on how his mother and father model the Holy Trinity.

Parents serve as representatives of God in the flesh until a child grows up and can learn to trust and depend on God directly. If parents reflect the unconditional love of God, the child will understand and have confidence that God will love him unconditionally. He will have security and confidence in God. Most likely, many of our children who do not love God had a wrong example of fatherhood or motherhood. Therefore, they project the idea of their mother or father on God, and that is why they are unable to love Him.

This kind of trust involves a fundamental confidence in God to keep us secure, regardless of circumstances. People who are in their thirties and forties talk to me about how their mothers left them when they were children, and how it still hurts, because they lost this feeling of security. Because of this, they feel insecure in their relationship with God; they feel that God may leave them, as their mothers left. If parents represent and reflect the unconditional love of God correctly, children will have the accurate perception and image of God. In John 17, our Lord Jesus Christ prayed and said, "The love with which You loved Me may be in them" (Jn 17:26). The Lord wants to say that the love in the family and in the church should reflect the love among the three Persons of the Holy Trinity.

A high level of primary trust is crucial for personal growth and healthy connections with others, which we call secondary trust. You will have trouble bonding and connecting with others if you lose the feeling of primary trust.

Intimacy

Attachment between God and us, or between people, is called *intimacy*. Thus, another name for secondary trust, or even primary trust, is intimacy. Primary trust is about our intimate relationship with God; we are in a trusting and confident relationship with Him. Secondary trust is intimacy between one another, like within a family or in marriage. Some people may think that the word *intimacy* refers to the sexual relationship, but intimacy has a much deeper meaning. It means being authentically known, knowing another, sharing one's soul, and being loved and valued by another. Of course, this can be applied to our relationship with God. When the Lord said, "I know My sheep, and am known by My own" (Jn 10:14), this exemplifies an aspect of intimate relationships: being authentically known and knowing another. Sharing one's soul is another aspect of intimate relationships, and that is why God spoke about oneness between Him and us. Lastly, being loved and valued by another is manifested in that God loved us to the extent that He shed His blood. This perfectly describes an intimate relationship.

Furthermore, the relationship within the Holy Trinity can be called an intimate relationship. It reflects the intimate nature of God, fully balanced and fully functional.

Trust in Marriage

God's design for intimacy in marriage means connecting with your spouse in body, mind, and spirit. This requires trust since you cannot risk your heart, emotions, and feelings unless you trust the other person.

Intimacy in Body

In the Book of Genesis, God said, "Therefore a man shall leave his father and mother and be joined to his wife, and they shall become one flesh" (Gen 2:24). This is intimacy in body. The same concept is repeated in Malachi 2:15, "But did He not make them one, having a remnant of the Spirit?" Here, he is emphasizing that God made them one, and they are no longer two.

Intimacy of Mind

Intimacy of mind includes friendship, love, respect, honesty, vulnerability, confidentiality, and healthy conflict resolution. It also includes sharing feelings, thoughts, values, joys, and sorrows. Adam and Eve were both naked and unashamed (see Gen 2:25). Nakedness here is not taken in the physical sense, but refers to the ability to uncover all your thoughts and feelings without being ashamed. We may lose this ability if at one point we became vulnerable, opened up, and shared our feelings, and our feelings were ignored. If this happens, we tend to start hiding our differences, as Adam and Eve did. For example, if a wife told her husband about a problem that happened at work and got emotional in the process, and he ignored her feelings and belittled the problem, she would cease to trust him. Trust would be affected, and it would be difficult for her to come to him again and reveal her thoughts and feelings. This is the relationship between intimacy and trust; if I trust somebody, I will feel comfortable to uncover all my thoughts and feelings without fear of rejection or fear of being ashamed. Many people do not feel comfortable opening up to their spouses. If this is the case, there is no trust, and we need to see what caused it to diminish.

Intimacy of Spirit

Intimacy of spirit means closeness of human experiences. It is a foretaste of the union between the Lord Jesus Christ and the Church. Since there is no other human experience more fulfilling than this divine style of intimacy, nothing is more painful than the breaking of intimacy and betrayal of trust, which occurs when a spouse is unfaithful.

Rebuilding Trust

We will discuss five points regarding how to rebuild trust if it has been lost.

Honesty

Say what you are going to do. Be open about this. Communicating your intentions to your spouse eliminates the guesswork that often leads to false assumptions and misunderstandings. Instead of leaving the other person confused regarding what you are planning to do, it will help the relationship if you are open and communicate your intentions, regardless of whether they are good or bad. To be faithful, to be trustworthy, you need to be honest and openly communicate your intentions.

Sometimes, I feel that there are mysteries between the husband and the wife. The husband may never tell his wife what he is planning to do, and vice versa. Then, they complain that there is no trust between them. Acting in this way will certainly eliminate trust. You should know everything about each other if you are *one* in body, spirit, and mind. Without this, how can trust be built? Tell your spouse what you are planning to accomplish, and how you would like to include him or her in your plans. This will certainly deepen the bond. Also, married couples sometimes complain about surprises. "Surprises" also weaken the trust between spouses.

Congruence

The first point, honesty, was about saying what you will do. Congruence means doing what you say. Do not promise something but then do something else. For example, if a husband wants to end a conversation with his wife, he may simply agree that he will do something specific, but in his mind, he is not going to do it. He merely wants to end the conversation. Consequently, trust disappears. When there are discrepancies or inconsistencies between your actions and your words, people will not trust you. The more your actions match your words, the more trust others will have in you. Trust develops when a person's words are congruent with his or her actions, which means that there is consistency. Say clearly what you are going to do, then do it. This will strengthen and increase trust.

Avoid Scorekeeping

Sometimes, people say to me, "I have been married for thirty years. Let me tell you what happened on the day of my engagement!" Live in the present and forget the past. When you keep track of how often a behavior has occurred and make a point of reminding your spouse of it, you drag the past into the present. This is called mental score keeping.

How does this affect trust? The weight of numerous incidents creates a strain that prevents you from addressing the current situation effectively. Scorekeeping builds stress, magnifies the situation, and interferes with the process of communicating clearly and directly about the present incident. A person may truly be trying to change, but if you keep reminding him about all his mistakes over the years, he will feel that it is hopeless; no matter what he does, he will never be trusted again, so he may decide to stop trying. Thus, this will affect the trust between them.

Accountability

"First remove the plank from your own eye, and then you will see clearly to remove the speck from your brother's eye" (Mt 7:5). Look at yourself first. Before pointing a finger at your spouse, consider your own behavior. Is there something you may be doing that demonstrates you are untrustworthy? Before asking, "Why does my spouse distrust me?" be accountable. Take responsibility. Are you doing something untrustworthy, perhaps even with good intentions? Are you giving your spouse reasons to distrust you? Explore the possibility that you are choosing a behavior that gives your spouse the impression that you cannot be fully trusted, and discuss this behavior with your spouse.

For example, a husband may never inform his wife about their finances. She may begin to doubt him, and he may wonder why. Well, why are you hiding your finances from her? Maybe he has good intentions, i.e., he is not doing something wrong, such as stealing, but why is there no open communication between them? If he knows that she does not trust him because he does not share the details of the financial accounts with her, he should sit down with her and discuss the issue. "When you say that you do not trust me, is it because I never showed you our accounts? I did this with good intentions, but let us look at everything together now." In this way, they will start rebuilding trust. Be accountable and look at yourself first.

Time

If trust is lost, you need to be patient; it will take time for it to be earned again. Time plays a major role in the development and strengthening of trust. Do not expect an overnight change in attitude from either yourself or your spouse. The more opportunities you have to demonstrate that your words and actions match, the stronger trust will become, but this takes time. That is why you should be sensitive and aware of all the opportunities in the future, so you can take advantage of them in order to build trust. Look for as many opportunities as possible to match your words with your behavior, and be mindful of your spouse's attempts to do the same. In this way, you will build mutual trust.

In conclusion, if you feel that your relationship is lacking trust, make an investment. Invest in building, strengthening, and maintaining your relationship by mixing these five points together. Put them into practice and support each other in your efforts. The result will be a relationship of mutual respect and connectedness built on a foundation of trust.

CHAPTER 5 Friendship in Marriage

The Need for Friendship

Two are Better than One

Friendship in the Family Helps with Five Human Needs

The Wounds of a Friend

Sharing All that is in the Heart

Barriers to Friendship in Marriage

Lack of Time

Losing the Feeling of Friendship

Not Talking as Friends

Conflicts and Differences

Using Hurtful Language

Protecting Friendship in Marriage

Make Time for One Another

Protect Your Friendship from Conflict

Learn How to Talk as Friends

The Need for Friendship

The family has a place in God's heart. When God created Adam, He said, "It is not good that man should be alone" (Gen 2:18), and He created Eve to be his wife. We read in the Book of Genesis that God Himself brought Eve to Adam and gave her to him: "Then the rib which the Lord God had taken from man He made into a woman, and He brought her to the man" (Gen 2:22). He also instructed them that they both will become one (see Gen 2:24). There is no bond stronger than this. The Lord Jesus Christ compared His unity with the church to marriage. When Adam took the woman from the hand of God, he said, "This is now bone of my bones and flesh of my flesh" (Gen 2:23), and St. Paul used the same exact words in Ephesians 5:30 to describe Christ's unity with the church: "For we are members of His body, of His flesh and of His bones".

This unity is important because, by nature, man needs support. He needs encouragement in his life. He cannot live alone; he needs someone else. Thus, God established the family so we can support one another. Family relationships have different aspects. There is a spiritual bond, an emotional bond, a psychological bond, and a materialistic bond. Also, between the husband and wife, there is a physical bond. In other words, there is spiritual intimacy, physical intimacy, emotional intimacy, and psychological intimacy. Numerous research has found that what people seem to want most of all in a spouse is a best friend for life—life-long intimacy. Friendship between the spouses or family members maintains family bonds. When we give priority and importance to friendship in marriage and the family, this brings happiness to the hearts of all the family members and is crucial for intimacy. It is not unreasonable to expect your spouse to be your best friend. It is just that friendship needs to be nurtured in ways that many couples fail to realize until their friendship is gone. There are many people who are "just married," but not friends.

Feelings of loneliness sometimes cause people to consider marriage. A person wishes for closeness and friendship with someone. When Adam was in Paradise, although he had no worries or problems, he was not content and felt a sense of emptiness. He longed for a companion, a person like him with whom he could talk, love, and befriend. God did not rebuke him by saying something like, "You are in paradise; how can you complain? You have no worries." However, God confirmed man's need for another to love and befriend (see Gen 2:18). Thus, we can say that a main reason for getting married is the need for love, the need for a fulfilling relationship with another.

This relationship extends for all of one's life; it is lifelong intimacy. It is very important for a couple not to forget that they are friends. Usually, before a young man gets married, he gets to know a girl and she becomes his friend. They talk to each other, share their problems with each other, and exchange feelings of love. Eventually, they get engaged and married. After they get married, little by little, they become distant from one another. They no longer share their feelings or open their hearts to one another. They become a married couple that has forgotten their friendship. In order for a couple to be happy in their marriage, it is very important that they nurture their friendship. Friendship is like a plant; it must be watered in order to grow and yield its fruit, which is happiness.

Two are Better than One

How do we define friendship? What do we expect in a friend?

Friendship in the Family Helps with Five Human Needs

Ecclesiastes 4:8–12 answers some of these questions for us:

> There is one alone, without companion: He has neither son nor brother. Yet there is no end to all his labors, nor is his eye satisfied with riches. But he never asks, "For whom do I toil and deprive myself of good?" This also is vanity and a grave misfortune. Two are better than one, because they have a good reward for their labor. For if they fall, one will lift up his companion. But woe to him who is alone when he falls, for he has no one to help him up. Again, if two lie down together, they will keep warm; but how can one be warm alone? Though one may be overpowered by another, two can withstand him.

And a threefold cord is not quickly broken (Eccl 4:8–12).

Solomon begins by describing someone living alone who is very rich and who works a lot, but he is unhappy because he does not have a friend. He says that this is vanity and a grave misfortune. In the next verse, Solomon emphasizes the importance of friendship: "Two are better than one." In the family, we find companionship, friendship, and people who help us. If someone lives alone and is upset about something, he will not find anyone with whom to converse or share his feelings. However, in a family, he or she will find a father, mother, brother, sister, wife, and/or husband. Not only that, but people who are alone feel lonely. However, if there are two together, they keep each other company. When a person has a companion, he can overcome the feelings of loneliness and emptiness.

Some may wonder, "What about hermits? How do they fulfill their need for companionship?" Hermits have reached such a high degree that they can fulfill this need through their direct relationship with God. St. Paul the Apostle says: "There is a difference between a wife and a virgin. The unmarried woman cares about the things of the Lord" (1 Cor 7:34). Through their direct relationship with God, they are able to fulfill this emotional need. However, most people fulfill this need through a relationship with another. Thus, the first thing in marriage is that the husband and wife provide companionship for one another.

Solomon goes on to give several reasons that two are better than one. The first reason is, "They have a good reward for their labor." This is about increased productivity. If someone is working on a project alone, his productivity will only be a certain amount. When two people work together, each one will be more productive, so their combined productivity is more than double what each one would produce independently. This is because one will make up for the shortcomings of the other, and they will complement each other. Maybe this is why the Lord Christ sent the disciples out two by two (cf. Mk 6:7; Lk 10:1). He did not send them one by one, even though, "The harvest truly is plentiful, but the laborers are few" (Mt 9:37). Lord, if the harvest is plentiful, instead of sending them out two by two and having them go to six places, if You send them one by one, they will go to twelve places. The same applies to the seventy-two disciples. If He sent them out one by one, they would have gone to seventy-two places instead of thirty-six. However, it is because they will have a good reward for their labor. Thus, in the family environment, productivity is greater than if each one was living alone.

When the husband and wife come together to plan for their life, whether it is their spiritual life, their life together in the world, or their children, their productivity will be better. For example, there will be a significant difference if someone raises his or her children alone as a single parent, compared to both parents being present and raising their children together. When there are two people, they will work together, think together, complement each other, and supplement one another's weaknesses. Thus, they will be able to raise their children much better than if only one of them was doing it. For this reason, it is incorrect when people call for divorce and claim that they can do a better job of raising their children alone. When both parents work together as a team, they will do a much better job of raising their children. [8]

The next point is about support: "For if they fall, one will lift up his companion. But woe to him who is alone when he falls, for he has no one to help him up." It is indeed true that we generally support one another in a family environment. If someone is lazy about prayer, going to church, or fasting, the other can encourage him. Not only this, but we also read, "If two lie down together, they will keep warm; but how can one be warm alone?" This refers to emotional warmth. We all need emotional warmth. By that we mean a kind word, praise, encouragement, and love. It makes a big difference. When spouses exchange words of love, this satisfies a real need inside the heart of each one of us. In marriage, there should be emotional warmth and fulfillment of a person's emotional needs. When there is love in the family, this love is satisfying to the family members. Being part of a family will fulfill them, and they will not need warmth from outside sources. This is why God stressed the importance of the family. As

---

8   These passages do not infer that single parents, whether widowed or having had to divorce, are incapable of raising their children alone or belittle their diligence, but there are extra burdens by doing the combined efforts of two dedicated parents by just one person.

human beings, we have many needs, which are fulfilled in a healthy family environment.

The last point is that there is protection: "Though one may be overpowered by another, two can withstand him. And a threefold cord is not quickly broken." If someone attacks another, he may defeat him. However, if two people stand against the attacker, they will be able to overcome him. If someone comes up against me, the family will be with me; I will find protection. This "one" is the devil who fights me. It could also be a disturbing thought or a problem I am facing. "The threefold cord" is a symbol of the man, the wife, and God, who is in their midst. When the couple is united with God, they cannot be easily separated. There is also a certain degree of protection that every husband provides his wife and every wife provides her husband.

Therefore, the family environment provides five things: companionship, protection, support, productivity, and warmth. God cared to instill a strong sense of unity in the family, in order for the family to be able to provide for all our needs, including these five things. Without the family bond, we would not find these five needs being fulfilled. Each person would be separate and living alone, and there would be no protection, support, warmth, productivity, or companionship. These are the things that spouses should provide for one another in marriage.

The Wounds of a Friend

Besides these five points, a friend also offers rebuke when necessary. We read in the Book of Proverbs: "Faithful are the wounds of a friend, but the kisses of an enemy are deceitful" (Prov 27:6). Sometimes, if it is necessary, one can confront his companion in love. This is what we call a "loving challenge." If someone sees you going down the wrong path but agrees with you, he is deceiving you. You may feel happy because he says what you want to hear, but, in reality, he does not love you. On the other hand, someone who truly loves you will tell you that you are going down the wrong path and that you need to turn around. Even if his words upset you, they will help you turn around and correct your course in life. A friend can sometimes wound, but

81

he wounds with love in order to help; this is why he said, "the wounds of a friend." The purpose of these wounds is to bring healing. It is like when a physician lances an infected area to clean it out so the patient can heal. As friends, the husband and wife should challenge each other in this way. If one of them sees the other begin to stray from the correct path, he or she should challenge the other with love.

When there is true love between the husband and wife, they will never be afraid to confront one another because, "Perfect love casts out fear" (1 Jn 4:18). In true friendship, there is no place for fear. A husband would never think, "If I say this to my wife, will she be upset?" Nor would a wife ever think, "If I say this to my husband, will he be upset?" If they think in this way, the love between them is not perfect. On the other hand, when perfect love exists between them, they will be able to share their honest feedback with one another without fear of upsetting one another. Because there was a strong and perfect love between the Lord and His disciples, He was able to give them feedback. He was able to tell Peter, "Get behind Me, Satan! You are an offense to Me, for you are not mindful of the things of God, but the things of men" (Mt 16:23). St. Peter did not get upset; on the contrary, he needed to be rebuked in order to turn his life around. Similarly, the husband and wife should be able to admonish one another when necessary.

Sharing All that is in the Heart

Friendship begins between a husband and wife when a person opens his heart and shares all his feelings with the other without fear. They become best friends who cannot hide anything from one another. In John 15:15, the Lord says to His disciples: "No longer do I call you servants, for a servant does not know what his master is doing; but I have called you friends, for all things that I heard from My Father I have made known to you." To Him, the disciples were not servants, because nobody shares his thoughts, plans, and secrets with servants. He considered them friends, and that is why He told them all that He heard from His Father. Here, the Lord Jesus Christ is emphasizing the fact that there is sharing in friendship.

A friend and a lover make known to the other all his secrets without shame or fear that the other will make fun of his opinion. When real friendship exists between the husband and wife, there will be no secrets or barriers between them. They will both be able to expose their hearts to one another and share their secrets, thoughts, and feelings. A friend is someone to whom I can bare my heart and share everything in it without shame. Do we provide this type of friendship as husbands and wives, or with our children? Can our children talk to us and share what is in the depth of their hearts? Do we provide this kind of environment?

Barriers to Friendship in Marriage

If we ask a couple who has been married for ten, fifteen, or twenty years if their friendship is the same as it was during their engagement or the first few years of marriage, they will likely say, "No. We do not talk to each other like we used to." It should be more but, unfortunately, this is not the case in many marriages. Perhaps, they are each preoccupied with other matters, work from home, watching TV, attending to household chores, or other matters, and there is no communication between them. They may say that they have nothing to discuss. There are several barriers that get in the way of true friendship between a husband and wife. We will discuss five barriers: lack of time, losing the feeling of friendship, not talking as friends, the presence of unresolved issues or differences, and using hurtful words, which cause wounds that remain unhealed.

Lack of Time

Perhaps, both the husband and wife work all day and come home in the evening. When they return home, they need to see to their children's needs, pay their bills, and attend to various matters, individually. They may want to go to bed early so they can wake up early the next day. In the end, they may not have time to see each other or spend time together, and gradually, their friendship diminishes.

In our lives, there are many activities competing for our time. How many times have you been in a bookstore, seen an interesting book, and bought it intending to read it? How many times have you read one page, then stopped, despite having a desire to read it? You never finish it because of lack of time. How many times do you think of a great idea, such as taking your family for a day out, visiting a friend, or doing a project for church, but end up not putting it in action because of time constraints? Unfortunately, friendship in marriage, the very core of the relationship between spouses, sometimes takes a backseat to the other priorities in life. These other things become more important than spending time with your spouse. Even though we said that friendship is essential to happiness in marriage, spouses often prioritize many other things ahead of it. If you make friendship with your spouse a priority, you will find the time for it.

[Please refer to Chapter 3 for more on lack of time.]

Losing the Feeling of Friendship

The second barrier is when couples lose the feeling of friendship and think that this is something for younger couples. Their marriage becomes like a business relationship: They discuss how to raise their kids, secure their financial future, go to church together, etc. Many couples these days are "just married," i.e., simply living together and dealing with each other so they can manage their lives and raise their children. However, most marriages began with a real sense of friendship and love. Many researchers have found that the happiest and strongest marriages are those that maintain a solid friendship over the years. For this reason, a husband and wife must nurture the feelings of love and respect for one another. Friendship is one of the main factors that help us stay connected.

In order to maintain the friendship, you need to maintain a deep respect for one another as friends who are able to share everything in an atmosphere of deep acceptance. Sharing requires acceptance. If I want to share something but I feel rejected, I will not share it. If one spouse wants to open up about something, the other spouse should be ready and willing to listen. Otherwise, you will lose that essence of friendship. For example, if a wife complains to her husband that he has not said anything loving to her in a while, he may respond, "Are you not too old for that?" Here, he is not accepting or meeting her needs; he is belittling her. Another example is if a husband provides his wife with constructive criticism in a pleasant way, and she does not accept it and claims that he always criticizes her. These are examples of lack of acceptance among spouses. On the other hand, when both spouses accept one another, open their hearts to each other, accept feedback from one another, and share loving words together, their relationship becomes strong.

Not Talking as Friends

The third barrier is the lack of friendly communication between the spouses.

[Please refer to Chapters 3 and 5.]

Conflicts and Problems

The fourth barrier is the presence of conflicts and problems that erode friendship. I want to tell you that a normal Christian family is not the family that does not have problems, but the family that knows how to solve and work out their problems. A husband and wife are two people who are different in all aspects, and they enter by marriage into one home and live together. Thus, we expect a lot of differences and conflict. However, some families know how to work together to solve their problems, so it seems that they never have any. On the other hand, some families do not know how to solve their problems; therefore, their problems remain unsolved and it appears that they have many problems. For example, say there are two families and each family has ten problems. The first family resolves nine of the ten problems and ends up with only one problem unresolved. The second family is able to solve only one problem out of the ten. Therefore, when you look at the two families, it will appear as if the first family does not have problems while the second has many.

There are two types of problems a family can face: Instrumental or Affective. Instrumental problems are financial problems, such as monetary issues, immigration questions, lay-offs, inability to find work, etc. Affective problems are related to emotions and feelings. For example, someone who is very busy or under a lot of stress at work may suffer from depression or anger at home. The way we deal with these problems is very important. If the family deals with problems incorrectly, it can weaken the love in the family.

Unresolved instrumental problems may make it difficult for a couple to deal with affective problems. In the Divine Liturgy according to St. Basil, we pray saying, "That ... having sufficiency in everything always, we may abound in every good deed." When a person always has sufficiency in everything, he will be able to abound in every good deed. That is why it is important to work together to solve our problems, especially the instrumental problems.

A family must train itself to resolve conflicts in a Christian way. The Holy Bible is an excellent guide for resolving conflict in a Christian way. If there are unresolved conflicts, dragging on for months, or perhaps even years, every feeling of friendship between the couple will be completely lost.

Differences between spouses should complement one another. However, we often let our differences cause us to clash with one another. As soon as clashes occur, feelings of love and friendship weaken, decline, or cease. We must learn how to work out our differences and use them to our advantage. When St. Anthony was asked about the relationship between monks, he said, "Love and humility subdue beasts." If one spouse has a difficult nature and the other spouse deals with him or her with love and humility, they can overcome the other's difficult nature. If there is true love and humility between a husband and wife, none of their differences will lead to conflict or work against them, but will work to their advantage. If we do not handle our differences correctly, they can lead to conflict and prevent us from being able to communicate with each other as friends. Sometimes, problems have no solution because we lose these two things. If love and humility are present, the beastly nature in us will be subdued and we will be able to live in peace.

Using Hurtful Language

The last barrier to friendship in marriage is lack of respect for each other and the use of hurtful language. For example, a husband may constantly insult his wife or put her down. How can friendship exist in this case? Having a different opinion or making a mistake does not give the other spouse the right to be insulting or demeaning. In Proverbs 12:18, we read: "There is one who speaks like the piercings of a sword." Someone may use words, jokingly, that seem like the piercing of a sword to the other person. A word that is like the piercing of a sword will wound the other person. A deep wound will require a long time to heal. These words leave scars and can destroy the feeling of friendship between the married couple.

When you insult the other, you are insulting a person who was created in the image of God, so it is like you are insulting God. For that reason, the Holy Bible says: "Whoever says to his brother, 'Raca!' shall be in danger of the council" (Mt 5:22). The same goes for your children. It is your responsibility to instruct your children, but it is not your right to insult them or say something hurtful, let alone to hit them. Who said that hitting others is acceptable or that it solves problems? Who said that hitting others is Christian behavior? Even if the other person makes a horrible mistake, it is never your right to insult or hit someone else. It is your right to say that something is wrong, that you will not accept it, and to take a stand, but it is never your right to hit your wife or children.

Hurtful words and disrespect create barriers between the spouses that cause feelings of friendship and love to diminish and disappear. Imagine if a spouse shares with the other a problem that happened at work, and the other says, "Nobody respects you at work because you are not a respectable person." If someone says something like that to me, do you think I will go to this person again if I experience another problem in the future? Certainly not. When we insult each other, we close the door to our hearts and our ability to share our feelings, worries, thoughts, and weaknesses with one another. If a son tells his father that he got a bad grade on a test, and his father insults him thinking that will make him a better student, that son will never tell his father if he gets another bad grade. On the other hand, if the father talks to his son, and encourages him to study and be successful, the son will not be afraid to share other weaknesses with his father.

Protecting Friendship in Marriage

We discussed five barriers that get in the way of true friendship in marriage. Now we will discuss how to protect this friendship. If you and your spouse are already friends, these tips will help you nurture and strengthen your friendship. If your marriage is lacking friendship, these tips will help you build your friendship. You will notice that these points are opposites of the barriers. First, make time for your spouse. Second, protect your friendship from differences and problems that destroy it. Third, learn and train yourselves to talk as friends.

Make Time for One Another

[Discussed further in Chapter 3]

The first piece of advice to help family intimacy is to make time for friendship. Friendship is time spent enjoying each other's company. It is important to have time like this between the husband and wife as a couple, and among all the family members. You have to completely avoid the temptation to bring up problems during this time. Designate it to truly converse as friends.

Sometimes, because our lives are so busy, we may not have much time to spend together. You should at least make sure that the time you *do* spend together is quality time, when you enjoy each other. However, if you do not see each other all day, then end up arguing when you finally see each other at the end of the day, what will the outcome be? Some people refuse to go home after work because they do not want to go home to arguments, problems, and misery. They may go to several other places, simply to avoid going home.

If we do not set time aside for friendship, we will feel lonely. Friendship provides one with companionship, support, protection, productivity, and warmth. If someone loses this sense of friendship, he returns to loneliness, like the man Solomon mentioned (see Eccl 4:8).

Making time for each other requires time management. Lack of time management is a source of many problems we have. We have no appreciation for the value of time. If we learn how to manage our time, we will be very productive. I compare time to a suitcase. When you are traveling and need to pack your suitcase, if you have ten items to pack and simply throw them inside the suitcase, it may not be able to hold anything else. On the other hand, if you neatly organize your items inside your suitcase, you may find that you can actually fit fifteen or twenty items inside the same suitcase. Time is the same. Some people let circumstances manage their time for them. For example, if a person is on his way out from work and someone starts a conversation with him, he may become delayed for an hour or more. If someone is on his way to church and receives a phone call, he may be delayed because of it. You cannot let any circumstance derail your schedule; you have to be the one in control of your time. How could you let a phone call make you late for church? We have voicemail. If somebody calls you and you do not want to answer the call because you are busy, they can leave you a message and you can return the call when you are available. If we manage our time effectively, we will find time to spend with one another. I believe that lack of time is due to two things: friendship in the relationship is not a priority, and not knowing how to manage time.

In order to restore the friendship, you should find and participate in activities of mutual interest for the spouses and for the whole family. This is something good that strengthens friendship. Also, going out and spending time in rest and relaxation is very important. In fact, it is a divine law. Sometimes, people feel that it is wrong to rest or take a vacation. However, God said, "Six days you shall labor and do all your work, but the seventh day is the Sabbath of the Lord your God" (Ex 20:9). God rested on the seventh day.

Moreover, in the Gospel according to St. Luke, we read: "Now when it was day, He departed and went into a deserted place. And the crowd sought Him and came to Him, and tried to keep Him from leaving them; but He said to them, 'I must preach the kingdom of God to the other cities also'" (Lk 4:42–43). This means that they pressed Him to stay and did not want Him to leave. However, He declined and left. The Lord Jesus Christ did not express guilt about leaving them. You may say here that He left in order to serve somewhere else. This is true, but look at these verses: "However, the report went around concerning Him all the more; and great multitudes came together to hear, and to be healed by Him of their infirmities. So He Himself often withdrew into the wilderness and prayed" (Lk 5:15–16). People were coming to Him to learn and be healed, but He would leave them and go pray. Rest for the Lord Jesus Christ is prayer, and He loves teaching the multitude. However, one does not replace the other; there is time to teach and heal their sicknesses, and there is also time for rest.

In another instance, He tells the disciples: "'Come aside by yourselves to a deserted place and rest a while.' For there were many coming and going, and they did not even have time to eat" (Mk 6:31). I am mentioning this because it is important that the husband and wife have time to go out, relax, dine out, and do something fun, something that brings joy to their lives and a smile to their faces. It should not be that you frown by default, and the exception is to smile. A person by default should be happy, relaxed, and having a good time. There is nothing wrong with having fun, as long as we are doing something befitting as Christians. We can participate in fun activities together, full of simplicity and enjoyment, and enjoy one another and the gifts God has given us. This strengthens the spirit of friendship between the husband and wife and strengthens family intimacy. This also applies to the family. The father, mother, and children should go out together, like to the park or bowling; they must spend time together in which they are relaxed and away from the tension and stress of life.

Protect Your Friendship from Conflict

When you spend time together as friends, you will find that even your discussions about problems will take place with love. This is why the majority of your time together should be spent in friendly conversation. How can you protect your friendship from conflict? First, set regular time aside to discuss your problems and conflicts. Do not be tempted to discuss problems outside of this time. You need to realize that you are not at the mercy of your issues. If you are discussing problems and concerns all the time, this means you are enslaved to them; the problems and issues are controlling your life, and you are no longer in control. You need to be in control of your life and enjoy it. Unless there is something urgent that requires immediate attention, things can wait until the designated time. This will help us avoid problem-talk at the wrong time and feeling ambushed by them. For example, if someone gets home after a long day of work and his spouse immediately starts telling him about all the trouble the children caused that day, this may anger and upset him.

We must exercise wisdom to know when and how to discuss and solve our problems. Do not be under the mercy of problems. As you need to be in control of your time, you also need to be in control of your problems. If your problems control you, you will never be able to resolve them. However, if you are in control of your problems, and you think about how to address them, you will have power over them and will be able to overcome them.

While we are discussing a problem, if we veer off topic and begin to fight, insult, or attack one another, we should stop the conversation because we will be unable to find a solution. Sometimes, people initiate conversations with me about a certain topic. The conversation begins smoothly, but, after a while, he may begin to lose his temper if he does not like my opinion. At this point, I say, "Look, right now you are losing your temper. We cannot continue talking because, no matter what we say, we will not find a solution. I would prefer to resume our conversation after you calm down." We call this a "time out." The same applies for discussions between spouses. We must learn to end destructive discussions immediately.

Another important point is forgiveness. Sometimes, we hold things against others for years, or even decades. All of us are sinners; nobody can say that he or she is without sin. All of us, at certain moments in our lives, hurt each other. If we are going to dwell on those moments, hold grudges in our hearts, and refuse to forgive one another, we will not move forward. That is why God gave us the commandment of forgiveness, in order to maintain our relationships.

We all need forgiveness because we are all sinners. If I need forgiveness, why can I not forgive others? Forgiveness is not a favor you do for others, but a favor you do for yourself. If you are upset with me and refuse to forgive me, I may not care. Your withholding of forgiveness does not impact my life in any way; *you* are the one who is upset and bothered. If you decide to forgive me, you will be the one to benefit. When God gave us the commandment of forgiveness, He gave it for our own benefit, not for the benefit of the other person. When you forgive your spouse, do not think that you are doing him or her a favor. You are helping yourself and putting yourself at ease. A person who does not forgive lives in a self-made prison of anger, hate, and revenge. When he decides to forgive, he opens the door of that prison and frees himself. This is why the Holy Bible says, "Forgive, and you will be forgiven" (Lk 6:37). When we forgive each other, friendship increases in marriage. However, if we do not forgive each other, friendship withers and dies.

Sometimes, people tell me about things that happened twenty years ago and they have still not forgiven that person. How do we call ourselves Christians yet do not forgive one another? Every time we pray the Lord's Prayer, God is asking us to say, "Forgive us our trespasses as we forgive those who trespass against us." Sometimes, spouses get divorced because they lose the ability to forgive each other. If they learn how to forgive one another, they will not get divorced. Forgive one another for the problems of the past so that the trust that upon which friendship flourishes is nourished. You are not going to be friends with someone you do not trust or forgive. If you really want intimacy in your marriage, you need to forgive and rebuild trust.

Moreover, it is very important to realize that what is told to you during times of vulnerability, when your spouse feels your love and shares a weakness with you, should never be used as a weapon during times of conflict. This destroys the friendship between the couple. Be very careful, especially with information that was shared in love while the other person was vulnerable and pouring his heart out, believing that he could uncover all his thoughts and feelings without shame. Never use this information to hurt the other person. This leaves a difficult impression and makes friendship difficult. If you learn how to protect your friendship and resolve your problems, you will have a happy marriage and enjoy your relationship with each another.

Learn How to Talk as Friends

Relearn how to talk as friends. Friends know how to listen to each other. One friend does not talk the entire time while the other remains completely silent; this would not be friendship. If you want to talk to the other as a friend, you must also learn how to listen as a friend. When you listen as a friend, you should not be defensive if you are criticized. Rather, you need to listen and be objective. Defensiveness creates a barrier in communication between spouses. When you talk to each other respectfully, objectively, and lovingly, you will not be afraid of the other person's reaction. The goal is not to insult or demean the other, but rather, to support each other, build each other up, and grow together in God's love.

Your friend is someone whom you love to see and with whom you enjoy spending time. It is not someone whom you always think about how to improve or change. Some people think about how to change their spouses. Why did you marry her? You chose her as she is. I am not saying that we should not try to help each other grow, but if all you think about is how to change the other person to fit the image you have in my mind, that is wrong. A person may want his or her spouse to have a completely different personality, although perhaps God accepts their personality. Why would you change it? You must remember that you chose your spouse just as they are. We need to change the things that are not pleasing to God, but we do not need to change the aspects that please God but do not necessarily please us. You never have a plan to change your friends. However, in marriage, some people wish to change their spouses, or they compare them to others, which is wrong.

When you talk to each other, learn how to relax and enjoy the conversation in love. Praise and expressions of love are important. St. Paul says, "Husbands, love your wives, just as Christ also loved the church" (Eph 5:25). God loves the church so much that He describes her using the most beautiful words (see Song of Songs). Words of praise and love must exist between husbands and wives. They are not just for young or engaged couples; they must be present even after thirty or forty years of marriage because these words nurture friendship between them. [For more on this, please refer to Chapter 8]

When friends talk to each other, they listen more than offer advice.

93

When you talk to each other, listen. Do not give unwanted advice. Maybe the other person is not telling you about a problem in order to find a solution, but rather to vent. We often talk to each other, not because we do not know what we are going to do, but because we need to get things off our chests. If your spouse is sharing something with you and you keep criticizing his or her actions, it will make that person irritated and uncomfortable sharing feelings with you. Practice listening to each other. "Let every man be swift to hear, slow to speak" (Jas 1:19).

In conclusion, friendship is essential to a happy marriage. Without friendship, there would be no happy marriages. Some people may wonder whether there really are couples that are happy together. Of course, there are; it is not unreasonable to expect to be friends with your spouse and to be happy in your life. God instituted marriage in order for the two to be happy together. When He created Eve for Adam, He said, "It is not good that man should be alone" (Gen 2:18), and He created her so they could be happy together. You should learn how to achieve happiness in your marriage through friendship. When we nurture friendship, we will notice growth in all other areas of life: spiritual, social, and emotional. As God said, "It is not good that man should be alone." Thus, friendship in marriage is essential for the growth and maturity of the spouses. Let it be a goal for you not just to avoid problems, but also to enrich your friendship.

6 Love in the Christian Family

Unity in the Family

Love

The Seven Characteristics of Christ's Love for the Church

Obstacles that Impede Love and Giving
Mistakes
Selfishness
Busyness
Loss of Respect
Wanting to Change Others
Seeing Negatives in Others
Problems and Conflicts
Inadequate Communication
Expectations

Guidelines to Problem Solving

Unity in the Family

St. John Chrysostom defined the Christian family as being a miniature image of the Holy Trinity. This means that the husband, the wife, and the children represent the three hypostases of the Holy Trinity. As the Trinity is one, the family also is united. He also explained that the verse, "For where two or three are gathered together in My name, I am there in the midst of them" (Mt 18:20) represents the family. When the husband and wife (two), or the husband, wife, and children (three), gather together in Christian love, the Lord Jesus Christ will be in their midst.

Therefore, we should perceive the family as one unit, bound together by love. "But above all these things put on love, which is the bond of perfection" (Col 3:14). Love is the bond that ties family members together. Consider two individuals who were raised differently and were in different fields of study, then got married. All of a sudden, the Church asks them to live together in the same house, to have the same goals, and to live the rest of their lives as one. It would be impossible for them to continue without the existence of godly love in their hearts, since there are many differences between them.

After God created Adam, He said, "It is not good that man should be alone; I will make him a helper comparable to him" (Gen 2:18). This verse means that God made man with a need for someone to help him and support him in life. Also, God told Eve, "Your desire shall be for your husband" (Gen 3:16). Sometimes, in a family, everyone wants to live independently. The father, mother, and children live together in the same house, but everyone lives separately and has his or her own goals and opinions. On the surface, they live in the same house, but they are not united. They are like roommates who live together, but they are not bound together and do not share the same goals. This is not God's intention for the family. God wants the family to be one. It is not possible for Adam to live alone; he needs Eve, and Eve needs Adam.

It is very important for family members to feel the need for one another and to feel that they complete one another. When God brought Eve to Adam, Adam said, "This is now bone of my bones and flesh of my flesh" (Gen 2:23). They are the same bone and flesh. They are one: "Therefore a man shall leave his father and mother and be joined to his wife, and they shall become one flesh" (Gen 2:24). This is the unity that ties a couple together in godly love. Feelings of independence in the family are very dangerous, even if there are no problems between the family members. Independence is contrary to unity and it is not the way a Christian family should function. It is usually more evident in older couples; they have raised their children and retired, and because there is no friendship between them, each one goes through the day independently, watching TV or reading the paper, etc. There is nothing that unites them, because the family did not develop with proper Christian values.

The proper Christian development for a family is to grow and mature together in unity. This unity originates from love. If the family has godly love, which is the bond of perfect unity (see Col 3:14), it will grow and develop together. "In whom the whole building, being fitted together, grows into a holy temple in the Lord" (Eph 2:21).

Love

There are different kinds of love, and we will talk about three of them. In the Greek language, these three kinds of love are distinctive from one another, and each one has a specific name. The first kind of love is physical love and is called "Eros." With Eros, one person is attracted to another due to physical (carnal) desire. This is a worldly love that aims to satisfy the physical desires of the body. A marriage built on this type of love will not survive nor succeed, because after being married for a while, one of the spouses may no longer feel satisfied physically and start looking for other ways or other people to satisfy his or her needs. This kind of marriage is threatened by failure and adultery, since the only thing that matters to the husband or wife is the satisfaction of their physical desires.

The second type of love, which is more honorable than Eros, is Philia, which is emotional love. This is when two people marry because they are emotionally connected, as a result of the understanding between them. However, feelings change frequently and, therefore, their love changes since it is based on their emotions.

A third type of love is Agape, spiritual love. This is how the Lord Jesus Christ loves the Church. In the Pauline epistle of the Crowning Ceremony, the Church instructs the groom and bride to have spiritual love for one another, the same love with which Christ loves the Church. "Husbands, love your wives, just as Christ also loved the church" (Eph 5:25).

Therefore, when we discuss love in the context of the family, the Lord Jesus Christ should be our example. The husband, wife, and children should love each other the same way Christ loves the Church. Let us see how Christ loves the Church and, therefore, how we should love one another in the Christian family. There are at least seven characteristics of the Lord's love for the church. I hope that each person tries to apply these characteristics to himself or herself rather than to his or her spouse.

The Seven Characteristics of Christ's Love for the Church

1. Christ initiated love: "We love Him because He first loved us" (1 Jn 4:19). Many marital problems remain unresolved due to the fact that each person waits for the other to offer love. If we follow the example of the Lord Jesus Christ, each one should try to initiate love without expecting anything in return. When God saw the destruction of humankind, because of His love, He emptied Himself and was incarnate to save us. He did not ask us for anything, but He offered us His love. By doing so, He touched our hearts: "We love Him because He first loved us." It is impossible to sow spiritual love (with the seven characteristics, which we will discuss,) and not harvest it back. However, if you sow emotional or physical love, you may not reap it back. The common complaint is, "I did something loving and got nothing in return." If we offer spiritual love, we will certainly harvest spiritual love in return.

2. Christ loved us while we were sinners. He did not ask us to

become saints in order to receive His love. On the contrary, He loved us while we were weak and sinful. Spouses often complain and say, "How can I love him (or her) if he (or she) is doing that? If he changes his behavior, I will be able to love him." The Lord Christ did not love us in this way. "For scarcely for a righteous man will one die; yet perhaps for a good man someone would even dare to die. But God demonstrates His own love toward us, in that while we were still sinners, Christ died for us" (Rom 5:7–8). He loved us and forgave us. This is unconditional love. Christian love is unconditional: You offer it without any conditions. This is the way God loves us and the way we should love in our families. If there are conditions, it is not love. We need to know how to love one another. Love does not keep a record of wrongs but always has its heart open to others and invites them in. Usually, we have a record of what the other person did wrong. This is not a forgiving heart. This is not a loving heart.

If someone is doing something wrong, it is not wrong to tell them. The Holy Bible says to admonish one another (see Rom 15:14). However, it needs to be said in a positive way, not negatively. For example, how did the Lord tell the Samaritan women that she was wrong? First, He praised her for saying the truth. Then, He told her what she did wrong in a very kind way; He did not attack her. He put what she did wrong between two statements of praise. First, He told her "You have well said, 'I have no husband'" (Jn 4:17) and He concluded by telling her "in that you spoke truly" (Jn 4:18). Before you want to criticize somebody, you need to think about something good to say. If you do not find anything good, then do not criticize that person. If I want to criticize you about something, first I need to think about something good you did and praise you about it. After praising you, I can say what I want to say, but not in a judgmental way and not in a way that attacks your character. For example, if your child lied, do not tell him that he is a liar; you would be attacking his character. However, tell him that he did not say the truth. There is a big difference between saying, "You did not say the truth" and "You are a liar." Saying he is a liar is a description of who *he is*, but "You did not say the truth" is a description of what he did. There is a big difference between describing the person and describing his action, judging the person and judging the action. Sometimes we say, "You are dishonest." That is completely wrong. We cannot just attack each other. However, we can criticize actions.

3. Our Lord Jesus Christ's love was not only unconditional, but it was also rejected at times: "He came to His own, and His own did not receive Him" (Jn 1:11). "O Jerusalem, Jerusalem, the one who kills the prophets and stones those who are sent to her! How often I wanted to gather your children together, as a hen gathers her chicks under her wings, but you were not willing!" (Mt 23:37). The Lord Jesus Christ did not stop trying after the first, second, third, or fourth rejection. He continued to offer love even though His love was rejected. He died on the cross for those who rejected Him. Moreover, He prayed for His accusers and said, "Father, forgive them, for they do not know what they do" (Lk 23:34).

    Please note that this is something practical; it is not just something we preach. There are families who live by these principles and experience the blessings of the presence of the Lord Jesus Christ in their midst. Imagine if everyone in the family were willing to offer or initiate love, to love in spite of weaknesses and mistakes, and to continue offering love even when rejected. What do you think this family would be like? We would be living in heaven, not on earth.

4. When the Lord Jesus Christ loved the Church, He took note of her needs and loved her accordingly. His love was not theoretical, but practical. People often say, "We love our spouses. We labor and work hard for them and for the house. I stay home (or I go to work) and take care of the children and the house," etc. We use these things as an excuse. This is love that does not observe the needs of others. The Lord Jesus Christ saw our needs and fulfilled them. He saw that we were held captive under the yolk of Satan, and He freed us from it.

Therefore, love must be practical. It should not be given based on what I see fit, but rather according to the needs of the other. Perhaps the way I offer love does not meet the needs of the other person. He may need another dimension of love that I am not offering. For example, I may believe that love is about providing financial resources, while the other person may need emotional support.

5. When God loved us, He "made Himself of no reputation, taking the form of a bondservant, and coming in the likeness of men" (Phil 2:7). To love, one must forget his honor. The Lord Jesus Christ offered love full of humility. Often, the ego becomes a stumbling block to love. Despite the fact that an argument can be diffused by a simple apology, it may continue because the person's ego does not allow him to apologize. Or, the person who was hurt refuses to forgive unless the other person apologizes. If ego is not put aside, it will hinder both the ability to apologize and to forgive. A person becomes unable to humble himself. Love is not like that.

   True love is when someone forgets his honor and his ego, and approaches the other person. That is what the Lord Jesus Christ did. He came down from heaven, became man, was born in manger, tolerated a great deal of disrespect, and lived in the lowest state for our sakes. He gave up His honor for the sake of love. Who among us could tolerate slapping, beating, cursing, mocking, and insults? The Lord Jesus Christ did.

6. The Lord loved us to the end: "Having loved His own who were in the world, He loved them to the end" (Jn 13:1). What does "to the end" mean? It means that this love cost Him His blood, which He gave up for us on the cross. A person sometimes says, "I am willing to sacrifice, but only up to a certain point." Compare this attitude with the true love of our Lord Jesus Christ: "Greater love has no one than this, than to lay down one's life for his friends" (Jn 15:13). This refers to the ability to give. The more love a person has, the

more he is able to give. If a person is unable to give, he does not have love. When St. Paul talked about giving, he said that the Corinthians gave themselves to God first, and that is how they were able to give themselves to others. That is true love: "And not only as we had hoped, but they first gave themselves to the Lord, and then to us by the will of God" (2 Cor 8:5). To what extent is a person ready to give and sacrifice for others?

7. Christ's love for the church is everlasting. It never changes. Love never fails. Therefore, true Christian love should be an everlasting love.

When we look at these seven characteristics, all of us may feel inadequate or deficient. Who among us can love in this way? God is love and love in its perfection is God. That is why love is infinite. No one can say that he has perfected love, because that would mean that they had reached the fullness of God, and God is infinite. However, the image of this perfect love must always be in our minds. We should all strive to grow toward this perfect image one step at a time. Even if you realize that you do not have any of these seven characteristics, the goal must be to grow in love. Day after day, each one of us should experience an increase in his or her love and ability to give.

In summary, the seven characteristics of Christ's love for the Church are:

1. He loved first

2. He loved sinners

3. He loved although He was rejected

4. He loved her [the Church] practically and fulfilled her needs

5. He emptied Himself

6. He loved to the end

7. He loved her [the Church] with an everlasting love

Perhaps these are the characteristics of love that St. Paul

meant in Galatians 5:13: "Through love serve one another." The ability to serve others is the ability to give and sacrifice oneself for others. "For all the law is fulfilled in one word, even in this: 'You shall love your neighbor as yourself'" (Gal 5:14). Therefore, loving your neighbor as yourself is the summary of the entire law. If you love your neighbor as yourself, you will help him, serve him, take care of him, etc. The Bible in one word is *love*. St. Paul continues and says, "But if you bite and devour one another, beware lest you be consumed by one another!" (Gal 5:15). This happens in many families. They bite, devour, and consume one another. This does not exist in true Christian love.

When we say that we should *love* one another, love here is a verb, which means that love is an action. Nobody can say, "I cannot love the other person." If God told us to love one another, this means that we are *able* to love one another. Love is a decision you make. You make a choice to love the other person. You can also make the choice *not* to love the other person.

Many people confuse love with the feeling of attraction or the feeling of being at ease with someone. However, everyone, through the grace of God because God is love, can love any person, even an enemy, if we want. It really surprises me that God asks us to love our enemies, yet we do not know how to love our families or our spouses. We need to learn, decide, and determine to love one another; that is what is going to keep us moving.

Obstacles that Impede Love and Giving

What are the obstacles that hinder love and giving?

Mistakes

The first obstacle is mistakes, either my own mistakes or the mistakes of others. I may not be able to prove my love because of the mistakes I make. How could you tell someone that you love her, then do her wrong? Therefore, your sin may be an obstacle for love. It may also be an obstacle for the person who loves you, because when you hurt her, you make it difficult for her to love you. Yes, we know that the

Lord loved us while we were sinners, but this is the perfection of love.

To overcome this problem, two things must be done:

1. We must train ourselves not to do wrong by the other. In this way, I can prove my love and help the other person to love me.

2. We must train ourselves to forgive others. As human beings, we all make mistakes. When we live in a family, we are dealing with human beings. We are not dealing with angels. We expect that the husband or the wife may say something wrong. We expect faults and mistakes. Therefore, when someone makes a mistake, I should know how to forgive. Forgiveness can solve many problems. However, sometimes, we are unable to love one another because our hearts cannot forgive. When we make decisions not to love and forgive, this is what leads to unresolved family problems. Mistakes remain alive in our memories and we are unable to forget or forgive. Without forgiveness, we cannot continue in our relationships. St. Paul says, "Be kind to one another, tenderhearted, forgiving one another, even as God in Christ forgave you" (Eph 4:32).

Selfishness

The second obstacle that interferes with love is selfishness. Love means going outside the boundaries of the self and uniting with the other person. If someone is focusing on himself and his needs, he will be unable to offer love. In the family, people often think of their own needs, and say: "No one cares about me," "No one is looking after me," "No one does what I want," "My opinions get ignored," etc. These statements all mean that I am only concentrating on myself. This is opposite to love and giving. In giving, a person forgets about himself and offers himself to others. True love means that a person puts others before himself. St. Paul says that love "does not seek its own" (1 Cor 13:5) but takes care of the other.

Busyness

The third obstacle to love is busyness. In the Western materialistic culture in particular, people are very busy all the time; they are almost in a whirlwind. The husband and wife work long hours. They come home tired or even anxious. Usually, there is no time to spend together or to have a light-hearted conversation. The atmosphere is always tense. Any conversation between the husband and wife or the parents and children is tense and stressful.

Because of this unproductive climate, it is important to dedicate time to spend together as a family in relaxation and enjoyment. It is always good for married couples to ask themselves if they are friends. If you want to unload or discuss something, can you do that with your spouse? Usually, I do not see friendship between spouses. They cohabitate, but are not friends. A friend is a person with whom you can share all your problems, worries, concerns, joys, feelings, etc. This friendship is often absent. You can overcome this problem by dedicating time to spend together in an atmosphere of love and peace.

Sometimes, when friendship does not exist within the family, family members start making friends outside the family. Occasionally, these outside friendships may be a hindrance to family love. For example, a husband or wife may search for friends outside the family with whom they feel comfortable and would maintain these friendships at the expense of their relationship with their family. Even if these friendships are with people of the same gender, they may sometimes have a negative effect on the family if they are stronger than the friendships within the family. However, it becomes a major problem if the outside friendship is with the opposite gender. This requires reconsideration, and for the spouses themselves to become friends. Family love should be the strongest bond. However, if the husband or wife search for friends of the opposite gender outside the family, this friendship will negatively impact family unity and can be an obstacle for love.

Relatives and in-laws can also be outside influences that affect love in the family, especially if they interfere in family issues. If the in-laws' interference is substantial, it can be an obstacle to the family's peace.

A family should balance honoring, respecting, and caring for parents, as commanded by the Holy Bible, with setting boundaries for them in order to not allow interference with the love within the family.

Loss of Respect

The fourth obstacle to love is the loss of respect within the family. People treat their colleagues at work, relatives, or friends at church with respect, but once they get home, their language completely changes. This happens frequently, and I am not sure why. The person says to himself, "If my family does not tolerate me, who will?" Who said that the family has to tolerate insults and disrespect? Why does this person not train himself to treat the family that he loves with the utmost respect? Do not give yourself the freedom to hurt others on the basis that they have to tolerate you. This is wrong. Many people put a great amount of effort in controlling their temper when they are outside. Once at home, they do not put in any effort whatsoever. When you talk to them about it, they say, "I just cannot control my temper." However, they do just that at work and church. If you have the ability to control your temper in various circumstances, you should use this same ability to control your temper at home.

I strongly advise you not to lose your respect for one another. There should be mutual respect between the husband and wife, and the parents and children. For example, sometimes, jokingly, parents call their children names. What is the purpose of this? Rather, mutual respect and expressions of thanksgiving and appreciation should be used within the family.

Wanting to Change Others

The fifth obstacle is attempting to control and change the other. The healthy alternative is accepting the other person as is, instead of changing him into a clone of yourself. In this way, there will be a chance to complete each other instead of competing with each other. Couples often want to change each other, and they criticize each other's behavior. It is much better to learn to accept each other, as the Holy Bible says, "Receive one another, just as Christ also received us, to the glory of God" (Rom 15:7).

[Pease refer to Chapter 8 for more on this.]

Seeing Negatives in Others

The sixth obstacle is creating a mental image of the other person and refusing to change it, especially when this image abases the other person. We may acquire a very negative image of the other person as being a failure, for example. Even if some of the characteristics may be true, we need to train ourselves to see the virtues and good character traits of others. Each one of us has some positive traits. I will be able to see the positive traits if I train myself to do so. In spite of all her weaknesses, the Lord was able to see that the Samaritan woman spoke the truth. If you notice that the image you have of the other person is negative, sit down and write down all the good traits the other person possesses. This should be a daily routine until your image of the other person changes. If you are unable to think of any, *you* have a problem, not the other person. You are unable to train yourself to see positives in others.

Problems and Conflicts

[Please refer to Chapter 5 for this obstacle.]

Inadequate Communication

One of the problems that may occur in the family is when our words do not reflect our actions. For example, you can say things that mean that you care about your spouse, while nothing you do shows this care. This creates confusion. Therefore, communication should be clear and direct. Often, when someone wants to send his wife a message, instead of saying it to her directly, he asks one of the children to do so instead of him; this is indirect communication. Or, he says part of what he wants to say and leaves the rest for her to guess; this is unclear communication. Many problems are solved when communication is clear and direct.

The other element of communication is listening. Sometimes, while the other person is talking to me, I am too busy to listen because I am thinking of my response. In this way, the message is not received, and we may carry on a conversation without understanding one another. Moreover, spouses may remain upset with one another for long periods of time due to misunderstandings. Therefore, a good exercise to help ensure that you understood the other person correctly is to paraphrase what the other person said before you begin speaking.

[Please refer to Chapter 2 for more on effective communication.]

Expectations

The last obstacle that hinders love in the family is having unrealistic expectations. Sometimes, one person expects more than the other person is able to give. When we expect a lot of things to happen and they do not, this may affect the love in the family. Therefore, before giving someone in the family a responsibility or setting an expectation for him or her, ask yourself the following questions:

- Does he have the ability to do this? If the answer is no, then you are asking him to do something beyond his abilities.

- Are the requirements clear? A mother may ask her son to clean his room; so, he picks up a few items from the floor and makes his bed. Then, she gets upset and yells at him for not cleaning the curtains! The requirements must be very clear.

- Is he convinced that the request is necessary?

It can be a big problem if expectations between husbands and wives, and parents and children, are unreasonable. Family members can inform one another of their expectations. For example, a wife can say, "I would appreciate it if I receive a card on special occasions because that shows me how much you love me."

Guidelines to Problem Solving

There are some broad guidelines we must keep in mind when facing a problem in the family to be able to solve it together. This way, it will not become a hindrance to love. First, try to understand the problem. When we deal with a problem, we often say that a certain person is the problem: "The problem is my son;" "My wife is the problem." This is wrong. It is possible for a problem to manifest itself in one member of the family, but this does not mean that this *person* is the problem. For example, due to certain reactions in the human body, one organ may develop a problem; a person may have an enlarged spleen or there may be diminished liver function. It is true that the problem manifested in this particular organ. However, the entire body has a role to play in this problem, in the disease that manifested in this organ.

Sometimes, we try to fix the person that we perceive as the problem, without considering everyone else's role in the problem. Even though the problem manifests itself in a certain person in the family, each one of us should understand what his or her role is in the problem. All of us should participate in solving it, without laying all the blame on one person, the victim. For example, if one of the children is stubborn, disobedient, curses, fights, or wants to leave the house, etc., parents often look at this child as the problem. Parents may overreact and threaten to kick the child out, overlooking the fact that what this child displays is actually a sign of weakness in the family as a whole. Therefore, it is imperative to understand that any problem that arises in the family is a problem that concerns the whole family as one unit, and is not this specific person's problem. If we understand this point, then everyone in the family must contribute to solving the problem. Moreover, everyone must change his or her attitude toward the rest of the family in order for the manifestation within this person to change.

In the book *Marriage and Family Life*, St. John Chrysostom mentions three points related to solving problems in the family:

1. The stronger your relationship with God is, the stronger your relationship with your spouse will be.

2. See yourself the way the other person sees you, not how you see yourself. This is a very important point. Understand what the other person expects from you. If the husband thinks a greeting card is trivial and unimportant, this means he is not

paying attention to his wife's expectations.

3. Correct your mistakes that affect the love in the family.

We will be able to maintain love in the family if we keep all the obstacles we mentioned in mind and try to avoid them.

7 True Joy in Marriage

A True Hero

Children have an image of what a hero should be like: A superman with power beyond our imagination that can rescue others from injustice. Adults also have this image of a hero, and this was the idea the people of Israel had in their minds. They were suffering under the authority of the Roman Empire and they were looking for a military hero, riding on a horse, to come and rescue them. However, the Lord entered into Jerusalem riding on a colt; thus, they were disappointed. They were looking for a hero to fit their expectations. The Lord Jesus Christ came as a hero, not according to our definition or understanding of a hero, but to set the good example for us of what a hero should actually be like. The Lord Jesus Christ came with a higher mission, to die for His beloved, His bride, the Church. That is why He came. He told us that there is no greater love than to lay down your life for your beloved (see Jn 15:13).

That is why, in Romans 5:12–21, St. Paul compares between the first man, Adam, and the first perfect Man, the Lord Jesus Christ, God in the flesh. In this comparison, both of them reach a point of danger. The point of danger for Adam was the tree of the knowledge of good and evil. This was a challenge, or a test, for him. What should he do? Should he break the commandment of God and yield to the deception of the serpent and the instructions of his wife? Or should he resist? For the Lord Jesus Christ, the point of danger was the Garden of Gethsemane. Should He yield to the seduction of the serpent and refuse to drink the cup and break the commandment of the Father? Or, should He take the challenge and be willing to die for His beloved?

Let us examine how both of them reacted. Will Adam accept Eve's invitation to eat? Or will he resist and try to save Eve? Will the Lord Jesus Christ accept His Father's will and give Himself as a sacrificial Lamb for His beloved? Or, will He break the Father's commandment? Both Adam and the Lord Jesus Christ had a choice: Either to sacrifice for the good of the bride or take the easy way out offered by Satan. Escape is the path of a coward and death is the path of a hero. Adam chose the easy way; he yielded and did not resist. However, the Lord Jesus Christ chose the sacrifice of the hero: To die in order to rescue and save the Church. Adam's choice gives us the excuse to take the coward's path in marriage—to escape and not sacrifice ourselves for the other. The Lord Jesus Christ's choice provides you the opportunity to be a hero for your spouse.

Submission and Sacrifice

Family interactions should be understood through the example and model of our Lord Jesus Christ. We need to have a Christ-like attitude in marriage. In life, in general, and in marriage, in particular, we should have the mindset of Christ. This is what St. Paul says in Philippians 2:5–8. I changed the words slightly to make these verses applicable to marriage: "Your attitude toward your spouse should be the same as that of Jesus Christ, who being in the very nature of God did not consider equality with God something to be grasped, but made Himself nothing, taking the very nature of a servant, being made in human likeness. And being found in appearance as man He humbled Himself and became obedient to death, even death on a cross." That is the attitude you should have toward your spouse.

The first point is that He made Himself nothing, and emptied Himself. A selfish person cannot empty himself or make himself nothing. A selfish person is full of himself. In a selfish marriage, husbands and wives demand their own rights. However, heroic marriages in which the spouses take the example of the perfect hero, our Lord Jesus Christ, reflect Christ who gave up His rights. The Lord Jesus Christ gave up His own divine rights in order to save His bride (see Phil 2:6). A selfish spouse insists on being served, but a humble spouse becomes a servant. The Lord "made Himself of no reputation, taking the form of a bondservant" (Phil 2:7). "The Son of Man did not come to be served, but to serve" (Mt 20:28).

"Wives, submit to your own husbands, as to the Lord. For the husband is head of the wife, as also Christ is head of the church; and He is the Savior of the body" (Eph 5:22–23). Many of us understand this to mean that the wife's role is to submit and the husband's role is to lead. Although these roles are biblical, I want to tell you that this passage is about more than the roles of the husband and wife in the family. It is about a relationship that is modeled after the Lord Jesus Christ and the Church. Both the husband and wife are instructed to follow the example of the Lord, because He is the model for both headship and submission. When it says, "Wives, submit to your own husbands, as to the Lord,"— "as to the Lord" refers to the example of our Lord Jesus Christ. Thus, this passage is about how to follow the example of the Lord Jesus Christ as the Head of the Church, and also how to follow His example as He submitted to His Father in order to save and rescue the Church.

Many people do not like the word *submission*. Many wives dislike the commandment in the Crowning Ceremony to submit to their husband and obey him as Sarah obeyed Abraham and addressed him *lord*. This was not written by the Church Fathers, but it is from the Holy Bible (see 1 Peter 3). Many women ask why we include it in the Crowning Ceremony and say that we need to remove it. However, if we take it out, we should also take it out from the Holy Bible.

Why do people hate the word *submission*? It is because being humble and submitting to one another goes against our nature. However, our Lord Jesus Christ emptied Himself, made Himself nothing, and became like a servant. Keep in mind that Jesus Christ is God. On the other hand, we are originally from dust—what are we going to empty? For God to become a servant takes a great deal of submission and emptying. In a sense, yes, submission is demeaning. These three words from Philippians 2:5–8, *nothing, servant, obedient*, are demeaning. However, the Lord Jesus Christ accepted to empty Himself, willingly and lovingly. If you submit out of fear, compulsion, or reluctance, it is not accepted. If you do it out of love, it will be blessed. Jesus Christ, the God of creation, submitted Himself to the Father's will and gave up all His rights, privileges, and glory as God. This was demeaning, but He did it willingly in order to serve a spouse who did not deserve His respect. We are sinners, and do not deserve His respect. Despite this, He emptied Himself, made Himself *nothing*, took the form of a *servant*, and became *obedient* unto death. God is asking us to do the same, not for our own fulfillment, but to reflect His heart. That is why husbands and wives can submit to one another in the example of our Lord Jesus Christ, not out of compulsion or fear, but willingly and in love, like the Lord Jesus Christ who was willing to save us. If we understand His example, wives will not have a problem with the word *submission*. The Lord Jesus Christ Himself did it.

Husbands are also instructed to follow the example of our Lord Jesus Christ. That is how they truly ought to love their wives. I also paraphrased the verse in Ephesians 5 for husbands: "Husbands give up your rights and be the hero for your wife, just as Christ was the hero for the Church and gave Himself up for her. Husbands, love your wives as Christ loved the Church." How did Christ love the Church? He gave up His rights as Deity and accepted death on the cross. The world's perception of a hero is a superman. The biblical perception of a hero is self-sacrifice and laying down one's life for the other. This is the Christ-like attitude in marriage.

When God entered human history through His incarnation and sacrificed His life to redeem us, He was carrying out the most heroic act of all time. In this process, the process of redemption, He set an example for us. He modeled what it means to have a heroic marriage through His marriage to the Church. When we set His example before us, we have a choice: Which way should we take? Will I do what feels good, what I think will make me happy, or will I do the right thing and take whatever courageous action is necessary for the good of my marriage? Each one of you needs to think about which choice you will make. Will you take courageous action, even if your spouse does not deserve your respect?

Joy in Marriage

God taught us how to love by the fact that He never gives up on His love for human beings, even when we rebel against Him and hurt Him with our sins and behavior. His marriage to us is so important that He paid the highest price possible to have it—He sacrificed His life for His bride. Do we value our marriage in the same way?

Why did the Lord do this? Is it because doing this made Him happy? In fact, at the moment of sacrifice, there was suffering; there is suffering in sacrifice. The agony that the Lord suffered in Gethsemane shows how distraught this sacrifice made Him. However, He endured the suffering for His future happiness: "Looking unto

Jesus, the author and finisher of our faith, who *for the joy that was set before Him* endured the cross, despising the shame, and has sat down at the right hand of the throne of God" (Heb 12:2, emphasis added). The Lord Jesus Christ wanted a bride and a marriage, and that is why He sacrificed His life. He could not have her without sacrificing His life, without being the hero. With sacrifice, there is future joy. This future joy should motivate us to sacrifice and follow His example.

How does one find happiness in marriage? We emphasized the point of personal sacrifice and endurance, but there *is* happiness in marriage. Marriage is about happiness. God said it is not good for Adam to be alone, and He wanted Adam to be happy. We do not gain happiness by demanding it or insisting on self-fulfillment in the relationship. If you do not make yourself happy through self-sacrifice and following our Lord Jesus Christ's model, you will never be happy. Many people demand happiness from their spouses, and that is why they are repeatedly disappointed. They do not know the true way to happiness.

Paradoxically, meaning or joy in marriage is not found by pursuing happiness or self-fulfillment, but it is discovered by practicing self-sacrifice. Self-sacrifice should be the point of emphasis in family interactions. We have many opportunities to sacrifice every day. Self-sacrifice means to sacrifice my own rights for the sake of the other. If a team wants to win a championship, every player must sacrifice daily by practicing and following the coach's instructions. In the same way, you have many opportunities every day to give up what you want to do and serve your spouse. If you do this, you will understand real joy. Your marriage will be satisfying to the degree that you sacrifice yourself for your spouse. This is the challenge of marriage: to sacrifice your momentary definition of happiness for the long-term benefit of your spouse. When you have a successful marriage modeled after the example of our Lord Jesus Christ, you will understand and experience true joy in marriage. You will glorify God, because your sacrifice will reflect His heart and how He loves His bride, the Church.

God's Message to the World

Marriage is not only about you and your spouse. God wants to communicate a message to the whole world through marriage. When the world sees how you love one another, you demonstrate how God loves the Church. Marriage reflects the love of God. Thus, God ministers to the world through marriage. Reflecting God's heart and following the example of the Lord Jesus Christ will grant you to hear, on the Last Day, "Well done, good and faithful servant" (Mt 25:21). As hard as it is for men to love as Christ loves, I think it is also difficult for wives to submit to their husbands as to Christ. However, by modeling this, you are actually preaching to the whole world. We may fail at times, but there is a difference between someone who is struggling and someone who is just not on the right path at all. You will have another opportunity to get it right, as the Holy Bible says, "Do not rejoice over me, O my enemy, for though I have fallen, yet will I arise, because even if I should sit in darkness, the Lord will be a light to me" (Mic 7:8, OSB).

Respect in the Family

Respect is important in family interactions. Respect is the core of family relationships and harmony. We find that many problems arise between husbands and wives either because of lack of sacrificial love or of lack of respect. A family is constantly changing, and respect can be practiced in each new situation to establish and continue a pattern of respect. Submission implies respect. Thus, if we want to summarize the two commandments given to husbands and wives in two words (husbands, love your wives; and wives, submit to your husbands), it would come down to *love* and *respect.*

Family members know when they are being respected and when they are practicing respect in return. When each person clarifies what respect means for them, this makes the guidelines for respect clear. However, sometimes these guidelines are silently put in place. When the guidelines are not communicated, the other person may not understand what respect means to you. It is better to talk about it openly; then, expectations are understood, and it will be easier for both to meet one another's expectations. Family members' communication should be honest, straightforward, and trustworthy. This allows them to ask questions about what is expected of them and to participate in setting those guidelines of respect.

We should remember that all of us are human beings, and sometimes we make mistakes. Thus, family members should be willing to forgive one another. "If You, Lord, should mark iniquities, O Lord, who could stand?" (Ps 129:3). God gave us permission to make mistakes and to forgive, so we should be forgiving if the other person failed to show the expected respect. By giving one another permission to make mistakes and forgiving one another, we will grow and learn how to relate to one another differently in a respectful way.

Support is very important when someone is trying to show respect and fails. Encouragement and praise should be given. Recognizing and supporting someone's respectful actions are good beginning points. However, failing to acknowledge someone's respectful actions may discourage that other person who is trying to change his attitude and develop a pattern of respect. We should remember that each person has his own understanding of the meaning of respect. Each person is unique and has his own style and personality. That is why we said that open communication and expressing expectations for respect are very important.

Do not give up. Consider each situation as an opportunity for you to learn how to respect one another. We should also teach our children to be respectful. If parents develop a Christian and biblical pattern of respect, this will be taught to the children, and likely to perpetuate to other generations.

The Lord Jesus Christ modeled family interaction by sacrificing Himself, emptying Himself, making Himself nothing, and obeying unto death. Love and submission should highlight our interactions with one another. Respect and honor reflect our love to God and to one another; these are the two great commandments. Love, submission, respect, and honor are given to us to bring happiness and joy to marriage. Without these things, we will not experience happiness and joy. Those who apply these concepts experience the true meaning of joy.

8 The Language of Encouragement

Signs of a Need for Encouragement

Testing Your Need for Encouragement

Practical Points to Help Spouses Encourage One Another
    Change Your Internal Perception of Your Spouse
    Change Your Language
    Learn How to Accept Your Spouse as He or She Is
    Spend Quality Time Together
    Do Not Take Things for Granted
    Avoid Comparisons
    Listen

One of the very important languages for couples to have, which is actually one of the five languages of love, is the language of encouragement. Every person needs encouragement. Unfortunately, there is a teaching that entered the Church that is partially true, but many of us take it to the extreme. This teaching says not to praise others because doing so may make the person fall into pride or make the demons tempt him. In taking it to the extreme, many of us do not say any words of praise whatsoever to anyone, lest they fall into pride or get tempted by the demons. However, if you study the Holy Scripture, the Lord Jesus Christ encouraged people and use words of praise. This means that we need to praise and encourage others, but in a balanced way. If you do it excessively, the other person may think that you are disingenuous, or, may fall into pride, and demons will indeed start to tempt him. That is why we need to be reasonable when we encourage and praise others. However, not to use this language of praise and encouragement at all is also wrong, because each of us, regardless of age, position, success, or self-confidence, needs to hear words of praise.

Signs of a Need for Encouragement

Sometimes, when we do not hear words of praise or encouragement, we start to seek these words indirectly. There are symptoms that reveal whether you need encouragement or not. For example, someone who wants encouragement may try to get attention from others either by speaking about himself or about his achievements. He may buy expensive clothes or an expensive car. A female may use a lot of makeup. They will do anything to get the attention of others. If you are seeking attention, either directly or indirectly, this may be because you need to hear words of praise and encouragement, and you do not get enough of them.

Another symptom of needing encouragement is when you are self-conscious about your ego. For example, after leaving a meeting at church, or during the meeting, you think, "What do people think of me? What is their impression of me? Do they like the comment I made, or not?" People who are too self-conscious are usually very sensitive.

If you joke with them, they may get easily offended and hurt. Over-sensitivity is a third sign that you may need encouragement, which is apparent in your inability to accept any comment or criticism, even as a joke. A serious criticism will definitely be very difficult for that person to handle. Also, it will be very hard to handle any kind of comparison, even indirectly. For example, in a meeting, if I say that so and so did something in a wonderful way, after the meeting you may ask, "What about me? Am I not doing my service correctly? Am I not doing it perfectly like this person? Why did you mention this person and not me?" This would indicate that you need a lot of encouragement.

When a person lacks encouragement or words of praise, another sign is jealousy and envy. I envy the success of others or their qualities that I lack. Usually, as either a jealous or envious person, I do not look at what I have but at what I am lacking and try to gain it, thinking that if I gain it, I will hear the words of encouragement and praise that I need.

Another symptom is that some people become perfectionists. They want to do everything 100% perfectly, because when they do it perfectly, they may hear words of encouragement and praise. Sometimes, we set unrealistic measures of success and achievement for ourselves; that is what a perfectionist does all the time.

Control is also a symptom. These people feel that they are lacking something; thus, they feel inferior. The more inferior or insecure a person feels about himself, the more he tries to control in order to compensate for those feelings.

Moreover, isolation can be a symptom. For self-protection, the person may completely isolate himself from any social gathering. This is so he can avoid any criticism or comparison, or because he will be seeking words of praise in such social gatherings and will not receive them. Therefore, it is better for him to avoid these gatherings altogether. He may try to justify this in a spiritual way, which is called *spiritualization*. He may say, "These social gatherings are ungodly. I do not find God in them, so I prefer to be by myself," in order to put a spiritual dimension to why he is avoiding such meetings and gatherings.

Another symptom is exaggeration. A person may exaggerate his achievements in order to hear words of praise or encouragement from others. People who need praise or encouragement may criticize others harshly. When someone criticize others, he presents himself as better than them. This satisfies his ego and need for encouragement. Another symptom is that he may feel down, depressed, or unhappy without knowing why. He may say, "There is something wrong. I am unhappy but I do not know why."

There are many other symptoms. What I am trying to say is that every soul needs praise and encouragement. Without these significant words or assurance, symptoms will appear in one's personality. That is why spouses need to provide each other with words of encouragement and praise, but in a balanced way. Do not overdo it, otherwise the other person will not believe you. Do not avoid doing it altogether, because your spouse may search for these words elsewhere, and this could be unhealthy and have a negative impact on your relationship.

Testing Your Need for Encouragement

The following is a test for need of encouragement. There are ten questions. If the answer is yes, you can give yourself 1 point. If the answer is sometimes, you can give yourself half a point, and if the answer is no, give yourself no points.

1. Do you always try to seek the attention of others and do you like being the center of attention in any gathering or meeting you are attending?

2. Do you always speak about yourself when you do something wrong, even if it is minor, and do you blame yourself excessively and feel very guilty?

3. Do you pay attention to what people think of you, and is their opinion of you so important, to the extent that you feel enslaved to their opinion? (If they say something good about you, you feel happy; if they say something bad, you feel down.)

4. Do you feel hurt easily and do you keep the feelings of hurt and bitterness for a long time, even if others apologize to you?

5. Are you jealous of others? Do you envy others? Do you think

about what you are lacking more than about what you have?

6. Are you idealistic or a perfectionist? Do you want to do everything perfectly? Is your standard for success sometimes unrealistic?

7. Are you a controlling personality who likes to control every situation, to make others feel that you are important?

8. Do you prefer to be alone and do you isolate yourself? Do you mainly isolate yourself because you are afraid, or to avoid any negative comments or hearing peoples' opinions of you?

9. Do you criticize others a lot, and do you use harsh criticism to make them feel they are inferior to you?

10. Do you feel like a victim—that people do not appreciate you or realize how successful and important you are? Do you feel depressed? Do you sometimes feel down for no reason?

If you scored between 8-10 points, you are over-sensitive and have a problem with inferiority. You need to face yourself, and perhaps discuss with your spiritual father, in to overcome this feeling of inferiority, lack of self-confidence, or low self-esteem.

If you scored between 5-7 points, your feeling of inferiority is mild, but you also need faith and confidence in God to alleviate this feeling.

If you scored between 2-4 points, you are confident and need to use this confidence every now and then to help you overcome the moments of weakness in your life.

I hope that none of you scored between 8-10 points.

Practical Points to Help Spouses Encourage One Another

If you find yourself not encouraging your spouse at all, what practical steps can you take to start encouraging your spouse and being supportive?

Change Your Internal Perception of Your Spouse

Start within your heart. If you really love your spouse, you will be supportive and encouraging. However, sometimes spouses create an internal barrier between each other for one reason or another. Because of this barrier, you cannot encourage your spouse because you only see the negatives. Even when you try to encourage and support your spouse, it will be fake and your spouse will know that you are using these words just to be politically correct. You need to change from within yourself. Try to focus on the positives. Make it an exercise. For example, say, "Tomorrow I will see the positive things about my spouse." At the end of the day, write these things down. Train your eye to see the positives.

A monastery is a closed community; it is like a family. One of the monks told me once that he had a problem with judging other monks. When he sees a monk, he thinks about his negatives and his mistakes. I gave him an exercise to write down the names of the monks and beside each name, to write something positive that monk does every day. By doing this for one month, his focus switched from seeing what is negative to seeing what is positive. Each one of us has positives and negatives. When this monk made this switch, he stopped judging others. That is what you need to do. That is what I mean by saying that you need to change from *within*. True change starts from inside the person. It refers to your perception of your spouse. If you perceive your spouse as a bad person and you think that you deserve better and that he has a lot of negatives, it will be a challenge for you to encourage or praise him or her.

Change Your Language

The second piece of advice is that you need to change your language and completely stop using negative words and comments. We are often quick to make negative comments. For example, a husband comes home and says, "I had a long day at work today." His wife may respond and say, "All men work like this; why are you complaining?" instead of saying, "I know you work hard, and we appreciate what you are doing." This first comment is negative and not at all encouraging. The opposite is also true. For example, the wife does not work so she can stay home with the children, and, by the way, staying home with the children is a full-time job with overtime. When her husband comes home, she says, "The children were very difficult today and gave me a hard time," and he starts to compare her with another lady and says, "So and so works *and* takes care of her children, and her children are better than ours. Why are you complaining?" These are negative words. You need to stop using negative words completely. Rather, show understanding and empathy. Empathy means that you see the world from your spouse's point of view.

Sometimes, the intention behind saying things like, "I had a long day at work today," and "the children gave me a hard time today," is to hear encouragement or praise. When one hears a negative comment, it is destructive to the soul, and it creates a barrier between the couple. That is why St. Paul said to let your words be seasoned with salt that they may impart grace to the listener (see Col 4:6 and Eph 4:29). Ask yourself whether your words impart grace to the listener, or destruction.

Let us read some verses from the Scripture to see how God, as our Bridegroom, deals with us. In Hosea 2:14, the bride mentioned was adulterous since this passage is about the children of Israel who worshipped idols. Worshipping idols is considered spiritual adultery, so the Lord is not praising a faithful, godly, and pious bride here. He is speaking about an adulterous nation that worshipped idols instead of being faithful to their Bridegroom. Nevertheless, the Lord says: "Therefore, behold, I will allure her, will bring her into the wilderness, and speak comfort to her." That is what God does with us. I am sure you know the story of the Samaritan woman and how our Lord Jesus Christ spoke comfort to her. He told her, "You have well said, 'I have no husband'... in that you spoke truly" (Jn 4:17–18). That is what we should do. "I will allure her, will bring her into the wilderness, and speak comfort to her."

Isaiah 43:1–5 says: "But now, thus says the Lord, who created you, O Jacob, and He who formed you, O Israel: 'Fear not, for I have redeemed you; I have called you by your name; you are Mine.

When you pass through the waters, I will be with you; and through the rivers, they shall not overflow you. When you walk through the fire, you shall not be burned, nor shall the flame scorch you. For I am the Lord your God, the Holy One of Israel, your Savior; I gave Egypt for your ransom, Ethiopia and Seba in your place. Since you were precious in My sight, you have been honored, and I have loved you; therefore I will give men for you, and people for your life. Fear not, for I am with you; I will bring your descendants from the east, and gather you from the west.'" Listen to how God speaks to us, His bride.

Keep in mind that with all these verses, the bride, which represents us, is sinful, has drifted away from God, and is unfaithful to Him. In spite of all of this, look at the language God uses with her. In Song of Songs 5:2, He tells her, "Open for me, my sister, my love, My dove, my perfect one." She had left Him outside. "For my head is covered with dew, My locks with the drops of the night." She responds, "I have taken off my robe; how can I put it on again? I have washed my feet; how can I defile them?" Imagine that you forgot the key to your house and you are standing outside, knocking and waiting; your head is covered with dew, the locks of your hair with drops of the night, and your wife is just lazy and does not want to get up and open for you. She is telling you that she has taken off her robe, how can she put it on again? She has washed her feet, how can she defile them? How are you going to address her? What are you going to tell her? Are you going to say: "Open for me, my sister, my love, my dove, my perfect one?" Look at how Christ deals with us. This is to make us see how much God loves us. We need to learn from Him. We need to learn how to be kind and speak comfort and impart grace to one another.

In the same Book, Song of Songs, He says to her: "Behold, you are fair, my love! Behold, you are fair! You have dove's eyes" (Song 1:15). These are very nice words. Sometimes, people do not know how to address their spouses, but observe how the Lord addresses us. In Song 2:14, she was hiding from Him, so He told her: "O my dove, in the clefts of the rock, in the secret places of the cliff, let me see your face, let me hear your voice; for your voice is sweet, and your face is lovely." If your spouse is refusing to talk to you, hiding from you, and avoiding you, what language are you going to use with him or her? Are you going to tell him or her: "Let me hear your voice? Let me see your face? Your voice is sweet and your face is lovely"? Or, are you going to scream, yell, and threaten? "If you do not talk to me right now…!"

The first exercise is that we need to change our internal perception of our spouses. The second exercise is that we need to change our language. We need to completely stop using negative words and comments and train ourselves to use supportive, loving, and encouraging words, such as what God uses when dealing with us.

Learn How to Accept Your Spouse as He or She Is

The third exercise that will help you encourage one another is to learn how to accept your spouse as he or she is and forgive his or her weaknesses. When you chose your spouse and agreed to marry him or her, I do not think you said, "You know what? This is a good person to fight with." You were attracted to this person. You loved him or her as is. That is why you decided to marry *this* person out of the millions of people around you. Then, why, after marriage, do you want to change this person? Why do you not accept him or her as is? Let us learn how to accept one another as we are, as St. Paul says, "Receive one another, just as Christ also received us, to the glory of God" (Rom 15:7). Let us learn how to accept one another. Do not try to change your spouse. When the relationship is one of grace and there is an atmosphere of grace, and the dynamics are dynamics of love, change will take place in both of you. Both of you will change for the better. It will happen automatically. However, do not try to intentionally change your spouse. This will create a lot of tension between you.

You need to accept that your spouse is a human being, as you are. This means that your spouse has his or her own weaknesses, and he or she will make mistakes, as you make mistakes. As you need forgiveness, your spouse also needs forgiveness. You need to forgive, as you are forgiven. Spouses often expect the other to be perfect, sinless, and without weakness, although they know that they make a lot of mistakes and expect to be forgiven all the time. This is unrealistic and unacceptable. If you try to search all the verses that speak about how you will be forgiven by God, it is in proportion to how you forgive others. With the same measure you measure others, it will be measured to you. As you deal with others, it will be dealt to you. Thus, it is actually very serious. If you do not forgive your spouse and accept his or her weaknesses, you are actually in a very bad situation with God because God will deal with you in the same way you deal with your spouse. There is no mercy on the Day of Judgment for those who are not merciful on others. Part of helping yourself to be supportive and able to say encouraging words and words of praise is being a forgiving person. You need forgiveness as well.

Spend Quality Time Together

The fourth exercise to help you use words of encouragement is that you need to have quality time together. Quality time is time to focus on the other person, and not on the duties of your life. When you were dating one another during the engagement period or just before engagement, most of your discussions were about how much you love her and how much she loves you. Conversations were focused on one another. Gradually, these kinds of conversations disappear and are replaced by discussions about children, finances, in-laws, etc. These kinds of discussions cause tension, because there are different opinions. If you are always discussing these issues, you will have no time to even examine how you feel about your spouse or to share how you feel with each other. That is why you need to stop and spend quality time with one another.

During this time, you need to examine how you feel about your spouse, and if your feelings have changed to become less loving, less caring, or less impressed by her or him, you need to examine why it is happening, and rekindle the first love. Do you remember when the Lord said to the angel of the church of Ephesus: "Nevertheless I have this against you, that you have left your first love" (Rev 2:4)? This can apply to spouse, since God is speaking to us as a Groom to His bride. Have you forgotten your first love, the first feeling toward your spouse? Why? The advice that the Lord gave is: "Remember therefore from where you have fallen; repent and do the first works" (Rev 2:5). Examine what happened, why this love started to diminish, disappear, or become lukewarm. You need to make a conscious effort in order to rekindle this love and friendship, and you cannot achieve this except through spending quality time together. Do not let the busyness of your life rob you of the joy of friendship and of a loving relationship. When you are setting your schedule, you need to set aside time to spend together. This time should not be once every month. I hope that every day you will have some quality time together, expressing your feelings to one another. This is very important to help you encourage, support, and praise one another.

Do Not Take Things for Granted

The fifth exercise is to try to observe what your spouse is doing and make nice comments about it. Do not take what they are doing for granted, even if he does something as small as bringing you some water or a cup of tea. The Lord told us that if you help someone with a cup of water, God will never forget its reward. God will reward us even for a cup of water we offer to a thirsty person or someone in need. I am sure you know this verse (see Mt 10:42). If God observes every cup of water that we give to a thirsty person or someone in need, you are not better than God. You need to be watchful. If your wife brings you a cup of tea, do not tell her, "It is cold," or "This is not good." Tell her, "Thank you." Be kind and note even the small things, and definitely the major things. Express how much you appreciate what she is doing and how you are grateful for what he is doing.

Also, observe his or her achievements and successes, and praise him or her for these things. For example, if your spouse got promoted, passed an exam, or made any sort of accomplishment at work, be attentive to these things, mention them, and encourage.

Avoid Comparisons

Avoid comparing your spouse with others, especially in a negative way by putting your spouse down and trying to point out how someone else's wife or husband is doing more than what your spouse is doing. This is very destructive.

Listen

The last point is that when spouses speak about their achievements or accomplishments, listen to them. By listening and paying attention to what they are saying, this shows interest and is in itself encouraging. Maybe their work is not interesting to you, or their achievement or accomplishment is not in an area of interest to you; maybe you feel that it is boring. However, if you think about it, you will realize that it is an accomplishment or achievement in something that your spouse likes to do. By showing genuine interest, listening, and paying attention, this in itself makes your spouse feel loved, encouraged, and supported in whatever she or he are doing.

I hope that we can reexamine ourselves. Each one of us should ask him or herself, "To what extent am I supportive and encouraging? To what extent do I say words of praise and communicate this language of love to my spouse?" As I told you, every person, regardless of age, position, or success, needs words of encouragement. We saw how the Lord Jesus Christ encourages, supports, and says words of praise and love to all of us all the time, despite our weaknesses and unfaithfulness to Him. Believe me, when you start encouraging and supporting one another, you will take your relationship to a higher and better level.

CHAPTER
9 Forgiveness

Two Porcupines

The Definition and Effects of Forgiveness

Responsibility

Unintentional Mistakes

Not Agreeing on the Nature of a Wrongdoing

Reconciliation

Trust

Seven Steps in Forgiveness and Reconciliation

Two Porcupines

One of the most beautiful analogies of forgiveness compares a married couple to two porcupines: There were two porcupines living in Alaska. When the snow began to fall, they moved close to each other in order to get warm; in other words, they were together. However, they started to hurt each other because of their spikes, and so they separated again, which caused them to get cold again. Eventually, they decided that they would stay together and accommodate themselves to the pain, in order to live in warmth. In order to live together while causing each other pain, they needed forgiveness. In other words, in order to keep warm, we have to endure getting hurt from time to time. Therefore, we have to learn to forgive one another. There are no successful marriages without forgiveness. There is actually no successful relationship between any two individuals without forgiveness. Perhaps that is the reason God made sure to include this commandment for us in the Lord's prayer: "And forgive us our debts, as we forgive our debtors" (Mt 6:12).

Every day, we are all exposed to things that can hurt us, or we hurt others. Examples of such things include derogatory remarks, avoidance, negative interpretation, cruel comments, rudeness, addictions to cigarettes, drugs, or pornography, making decisions without regarding the needs of others, or forgetting matters of significance such as Mother's Day or your wife's birthday. Some jokingly say that the best way to remember your wife's birthday is to forget it once. Unfortunately, I have noticed that in the last few years, rudeness has increased. In the past, people used to deal with each other with respect, even if they disagreed. Now, dealing with others rudely has almost become the norm. Is this the effect of movies and the media? After all, rudeness makes people laugh. People insult each other, belittle each other, and humiliate each other in the name of comedy. However, impoliteness can hurt.

While the list can go on and on, we need to know that both spouses are imperfect and you *will* hurt one another, intentionally or unintentionally. However, keep in mind that the more significant the hurt, the more effort needed to move forward and leave the situation behind. The deeper the wound, the more spiritual and psychological effort is needed to put this event in the past. For example, if a husband threw away something that was important to his wife, that is not the same as committing adultery. Forgiving adultery takes much more spiritual and psychological effort and time, from both spouses, than in the case of one spouse throwing away something important or of sentimental value.

The Definition and Effects of Forgiveness

The word *forgive* is a verb. Therefore, forgiveness is not an ability, but a positive action. It is a decision to give up your perceived or actual right to get even with or to hold in debt somebody who wronged you. God always likened forgiveness to debt: "There was a certain creditor who had two debtors. One owed five hundred denarii, and the other fifty. And when they had nothing with which to repay, he freely forgave them both" (Lk 7:41–42). In the same way, when someone hurts me, he becomes indebted to me. When we apologize, we even sometimes say, "I owe you." Forgiveness is to give up this right. Forgiveness is to tear up the bill (of the debt), so that the person no longer owes me anything and he or she is free, as the Lord Jesus Christ tore the handwriting of our sins on the cross. He set us free, and told us, "You are no longer in debt because I paid it off for you." Therefore, forgiveness is an action, something you decide to do.

What would happen if you decided not to forgive? You would be unable to deal with the other person as a team, as one unit, since the other person still has a debt to pay. However, when you truly forgive the other person, the unity and oneness of the marriage becomes stronger and, at the same time, you fulfill the commandment of the Lord Jesus Christ: "Whenever you stand praying, if you have anything against anyone, forgive him, that your Father in heaven may also forgive you your trespasses. But if you do not forgive, neither will your Father in heaven forgive your trespasses" (Mk 11:25–26). When I forgive, God will forgive me. Therefore, to refuse to forgive not only means that you will create a barrier between you and your spouse, but also that you are creating a barrier between you and God.

Lack of forgiveness creates resentment, bitterness, and feelings of despair inside *you*. That is why forgiveness is a favor, or a virtue, done for oneself, not for the other. For example, if I hurt you and you decided not to forgive me, perhaps I will happily go on with my life, without caring whether or not you forgive me. However, you are the one who is hurt and full of bitterness. We agreed that forgiveness is like a debt, so we can extend this and say that I deceived you, stole a large sum of money and ran off with it, and I am happily living my life. (I will only be happy on earth, of course. I would not be happy in heaven, but I am concentrating on the one wronged in this example.) You, however, are very upset and angry because of the money I stole and ran away with it. Then what? This anger will give you ulcers, diabetes, and high blood pressure. However, if you decided to let it go and forgive the debt, *you* would feel much better. We will discuss what the person at fault should do later; I am not trying to say that people should simply continue hurting others while the others forgive. The point here is that when you forgive, *you* will feel better, and if you do not forgive, you are the one who will be upset and hurt.

A different scenario occurs when the person at fault does not run away with the debt, but sincerely apologizes to you once, twice, or three times, and is willing to do whatever it takes to fix things and reconcile. However, you still refuse to forgive. What would a person who felt unable to pay off his debt do? He would file for bankruptcy, since he cannot pay, and this is what happens. People often walk away from debts that they see no hope of paying off. People lose hope when they try to please the other person and obtain forgiveness by any means, but the other person refuses to forgive. This is what the Lord said, "Let him be to you like a heathen and a tax collector" (Mt 18:17). What can you do? You tried to apologize several times but to no avail, so let it be as he wishes.

When someone refuses to forgive, he will have certain feelings inside him, which may or may not be expressed verbally. Some examples are: "I will make you pay for what you did," "I will never let this issue go," "You owe me and I *will* get even," "Never think that I will forget what you did. I will remember until the end of my life, or until the end of your life." If feelings such as these exist inside you, it means that you have not forgiven the other person. Perhaps you do not verbalize these feelings, but you may express them by your behavior and attitude. This is called being *passive-aggressive*. It is when you do not greet the person or you ignore him, and other things such as this. There are many actions that can reveal the grudge that exists in your heart.

When we forgive, we force the devil out of our lives, and when we do not forgive, we invite the devil into our homes. If you do not forgive your spouse for one night, you invite the devil into your house for one night. If you do not forgive your spouse for one week, you invite the devil into your house for one week. If you do not forgive your spouse for one month, you invite the devil into your house for one month. If you do not forgive your spouse for years, you have given the devil a green card for permanent residency. This is what St. Paul the Apostle says in Ephesians 4:26–27, "'Be angry, and do not sin': do not let the sun go down on your wrath, nor give place to the devil." If you are angry, do not let the sun set while you are still angry; try to reconcile before the sun sets. He continues by saying, "nor give place to the devil," which means that if the sun sets on your wrath, you have given the devil a place in your home—you have provided him with an opportunity to dwell with you. Every night you go to bed angry at each other, know for sure that the devil is a guest in your home that night.

Some people confuse forgiveness with other things, and live with feelings of guilt without knowing whether or not they have truly forgiven the other person. I know there is a famous picture of the Lord Jesus Christ with a subscript that reads, "When I forgive, I forget." This is correct, but this is God. "For as the heavens are high above the earth, so great is His mercy toward those who fear Him; as far as the east is from the west, so far has He removed our transgressions from us" (Ps 103:11–12). If *we* still remember an offense, does this mean that we have not forgiven the other person? In reality, forgiveness is *not* forgetting. If I get injured, I can release you from the debt and no longer expect anything from you. However, the wound still exists and causes me pain. Also, no one can erase his or her memory. There is no verse in the Holy Bible that says, "When I forgive, I forget." This is merely a saying. *Forget* in this picture means, "I will not hold it against you." It does not mean that it has been erased from memory. In the same way, if you remember the event or even still feel the pain, as long as you are not holding it against the other person and constantly reminding him about it, this is normal and natural.

The healing that you are seeking here comes from God, since you no longer want anything from the other person; you have given up your rights in regards to the other person. However, you are asking for healing from God. Therefore, forgiveness is different from feeling the effect of an offense. For example, a wife may forgive her husband because he cheated on her. She is not holding it against him, nor does she talk about it with him. However, every now and then, this subject crosses her mind; this is normal. Every now and then, this subject causes her pain, and that, too, is normal. I cannot say that if she remembers or feels some pain, that she did not forgive her husband, unless she always reminds him about it, whether directly or indirectly. Reminding him indirectly would entail being passive aggressive (frowning, being upset, not wanting to talk, etc.). In this case, perhaps she avoids talking about it so that she does not reveal she has yet to forgive him, but she acts out the anger and resentment.

If there are still memories and pain, we go to God, the true Physician. We pray in the Divine Liturgy for God to "Cleanse us from … the remembrance of vice bearing death" (Divine Liturgy according to St. Basil). Thus, we will not bring up or rehash the same event or subject over and over again. We will be able to keep it in the past and stop it from ruining the present.

Responsibility

Does forgiving the other person mean that he or she is no longer responsible for what they did? No, it does not mean this. There is a difference between giving up your rights and the other person's responsibility for the wrong or hurt he or she caused you. Recall the story we mentioned earlier about the person who stole money and ran away. Even if I forgive and give up my right, this does not excuse him from the responsibility of correcting his mistake. He is still responsible for paying the debt. Yes, I do not expect it, but he is still responsible.

This is not meant for the person who was hurt and forgave. This is for the party that was at fault, whom the other side forgave. If you are the one at fault and the other person sincerely forgave you, do not think this means you are not responsible for your wrongdoing and for correcting it. Zacchaeus (Lk 19:1–10) cheated many people. These people could not ask for their rights because Zacchaeus was powerful and strong. Perhaps some of them forgave him and forgot about what happened. However, this did not excuse Zacchaeus from his responsibility toward the people of whom he cheated and took advantage. That was why when God touched Zacchaeus' heart and he repented, Zacchaeus himself said, "Look, Lord, I give half of my goods to the poor; and if I have taken anything from anyone by false accusation, I restore fourfold" (Lk 19:8).

Forgiveness does not excuse the person from doing his or her part in taking responsibility for the mistake or wrongdoing. That is actually the reason we confess. Protestant doctrine says that the Lord Jesus Christ forgave our sins on the cross so there is no need for confession. Essentially, what they are saying is that because Jesus forgave you, you are not responsible for what you do. Of course, that is not correct. Who said that forgiveness excuses anyone from responsibility? Indeed, no matter what anyone does, he or she will never be able to pay off the debt of their sins. However, at least when I come and confess my sins and say, "Yes, Lord, I have sinned against you, and you, Oh Lord, carried the cross on my behalf," this confession is a way of accepting responsibility.

Unintentional Mistakes

What if someone makes an unintentional mistake? For example, if one spouse had something extremely important, very meaningful, and of great sentimental value, and the other spouse threw it out by mistake, how could we deal with that? A mistake occurred, but it was unintentional, and the other spouse got upset. If the person who made the mistake says, "I did not mean it," and refuses to apologize or comfort the other person, this is not right. Despite the fact that it was unintentional, and we have no doubt that you were not doing it to hurt the other person, this unintentional mistake still caused the other person pain. Because you hurt the other person, you need to apologize. If you were driving your car and hit someone unintentionally, would you not get out of your car and apologize? You were not driving recklessly or anything, but you hit him and injured him. Would you just say, "I was following the rules, so I am not responsible for your injury?" No, you injured him.

It is important to realize that you must apologize if an unintentional mistake occurs. Also, the person who got hurt must not be over-dramatic, but accept the apology and let the event pass since it was unintentional. In this way, both of you meet halfway; the person who makes the unintentional mistake apologizes and the other person accepts the apology without worsening the situation.

Not Agreeing on the Nature of a Wrongdoing

There is another type of situation that is more difficult. Suppose both of you are not in agreement on the nature of the mistake. One sees it as wrong and painful, and the other sees it as a right decision and thinks that his spouse is negatively interpreting it. For example, on Mother's Day, a husband goes to see his mother and takes her out to spend a few hours with her to celebrate Mother's Day. Then, he goes home to spend the rest of the day celebrating Mother's Day with his wife. The wife gets hurt because he celebrated with his mother before celebrating with her. At the same time, he believes that what he did was right. Here, one says, "I am hurt," and the other says, "No, I did not hurt you."

This is different from the first example in which someone hurts the other unintentionally. In the first example, they agree that there is a wound, but in the second situation they do not agree that there is a wound. This scenario is sometimes difficult to resolve because each one sees the situation from a different perspective. However, we need to remember the verse that says, "Blessed are the peacemakers, for they shall be called sons of God" (Mt 5:9). One of them must be a peacemaker and comfort the other person, without disregarding the truth. In the above-mentioned story, if the husband is a peacemaker, he can tell his wife, "I am sorry if this upsets you, but I think honoring father and mother does not interfere with my love toward you. I still believe that honoring my mother on this special day should not hurt you. However, I am upset because you say that you are hurt; I do not like for your feelings to be hurt. However, we can pray together for our relationship and for our relationship with our parents to be according to God's will." Here, he comforts her and shows her how much it means to him that she is hurt because of something like that and that he does not like to see her hurt. At the same time, he explains that honoring one's parents is a biblical commandment and a blessing we should strive to have in our lives.

Unfortunately, when we deal with controlling or unreasonable people, this approach does not work. Do not reason with an unreasonable person. If the other person is irrational, reason or logic will not work; logic works with someone who is willing to accept it and who can reason. Also, controlling and unreasonable personalities are the two most difficult personalities. They may need assertiveness and boundaries, and the reason for this is not to punish them but to lead them to salvation. Setting assertive boundaries is effective with unreasonable or controlling people. This is a big topic, which needs to be discussed separately; however, here we are talking about what you can do when your spouse is like the average person. [*The topic of controlling personalities is discussed in Book II [Understanding Oneself in Marriage] of this Counseling Series II on Marriage*]

If the wife is really upset that her husband spent time with his mother before her, she needs to examine herself and find out why this upset her, since it should not. What kind of insecurities exist within her? Is it the "straw that broke the camel's back?" Have things been accumulating? Does she feel that he puts his family before her *all* the time? Does she think that he gives them more attention than he gives her *all* the time? Is this the right day and the right occasion to create a conflict? One should have wisdom and know the right time to discuss an issue. I should not choose to fight about his mother on Mother's Day. If I do, even Abouna will not agree with me. Therefore, it is not wise to choose an event like that and create a conflict. If he really is putting his family before you all the time, express your feelings without fighting and choose some other event that makes sense for your point.

As we mentioned, it is a challenge when both of you do not agree on the nature of the mistake. Here, we need wisdom, the fear of God, and for someone to be a peacemaker so that we can overcome this challenge without giving the devil a place among us.

To summarize, forgiveness does not equal forgetting. Forgiveness is different than feeling pain; you can forgive someone, but still feel pain. Forgiveness does not mean that the other side is not responsible for his mistake.

Reconciliation

Moreover, forgiveness is not the same as reconciliation or restoration. Forgiveness is a step toward reconciliation and restoration, because we cannot reconcile without forgiveness, but they are not the same. On the cross, the Lord Jesus Christ forgave everyone, but He did not reconcile with everyone. This forgiveness certainly prepared the way for reconciliation and restoration; however, some people reconciled with God while others refused.

When the person at fault takes no responsibility to change the pattern of sin, reconciliation becomes much harder. For example, someone curses, gets angry, or is involved in sinful relationships, and the other side forgives. However, this person does not show any remorse and is not willing to correct this mistake. He says, "This is the way I am!"

The Holy Bible does not tell us to let this situation go, but rather to confront it. "If your brother sins against you, go and tell him his fault" (Mt 18:15), but confront him in steps. The first step is to "go and tell him his fault between you and him alone" (Mt 18:15). If that does not work, "Take with you one or two more, that 'by the mouth of two or three witnesses every word may be established'" (Mt 18:16). If that does not work, "tell it to the church" (Mt 18:17). Even this step will not work with some people, and that is why it then says, "But if he refuses even to hear the church, let him be to you like a heathen and a tax collector" (Mt 18:17). Forgiveness is unconditional. God forgave everyone on the cross. However, for God to reconcile with us, we have to accept responsibility for our mistakes.

Here, I want to warn you about something important. Do not be the plaintiff and the judge at the same time. You cannot say that your husband is like the heathen and a tax collector, or keep searching until you find a priest who tells you that your husband is like the heathen and the tax collector. A person may go to a priest who tells her that she is actually the one at fault. She does not like the answer, so she goes to another priest who also tells her that she is wrong. Again, she does not like the answer, so she goes to a third priest who tells her that her husband is wrong. Then, she thinks she has found a living saint of God on earth and decides that this priest is the one who will solve her problem.

Of course, Abouna reacts according to how you present the problem to him. Consulting more than one priest about the same problem is not beneficial for you. St. John Climacus says something very beautiful about fathers of confession in his book, *The Ladder of Divine Ascent*. It applies to family problems as well. He says, "Be very careful in choosing your father of confession, lest you fall in with someone who is sick, and not with a doctor. Then, once you choose him, never doubt him." When you have a problem, be very careful about to whom you take this problem. However, once you choose a particular father of confession, do not change him. We see this sometimes—families go from priest to priest about the same problem. Why? Everyone wants a priest who will tell him what he wants to hear. You will never find the right solution this way. Focus on one father of confession, pray that God gives him the right guidance, accept his guidance, and continue with him. Frequently moving from one priest to another is very harmful.

Someone may ask, "Is it not the same Holy Spirit who speaks in the same way with all fathers of confession?" This is correct, but when someone wants to hear what *he wants*, God sometimes allows it. This happened with the children of Israel when they wanted to have a king. Samuel told them that God said no, but they did not like that, so God told Samuel to give them a king and that they had not rejected Samuel but God Himself (see 1 Sam 8:6–9). Sometimes, God lets you hear what you want to hear, not because this is God's will, but because of the hardness of the person's heart and his insistence on hearing something in particular. Therefore, God can let you hear it on the mouth of a priest or even a bishop. "Is this what you want? Here it is." Then, you go around saying, "Abouna told me this," or,

"Sayedna[9] told me that." It is like if your son comes to you and tells you, "I want this and this and this," etc. Eventually, you tell him to just go do whatever he wants to do. God does the same thing with us. "Go do what you want, since you do not want to do what I told you to do." Be careful that the devil does not confuse you while you are going around to different priests, and make you think, "Abouna [or Sayedna] told me, so this is God's voice to me."

Trust

Trust can be lost with pain. The deeper the wound, the more trust is lost. For example, if two people fight because one forgot something, such as an important meeting, this is different than being upset because of adultery. Keep in mind that trust will take time to rebuild. Trust builds slowly over time. However, trust will definitely return, and return quicker, if each spouse assumes his or her correct responsibility and role. On the other hand, if one does not care, disregards the other person's feelings, or does not accept responsibility for his wrongdoing, this may obstruct the return of trust. Also, since there is a relationship between trust and commitment, if trust does not return, commitment, especially dedicated commitment, will weaken. This is a cycle where the couple is living together in constraint commitment.

Therefore, if you are the person at fault, you need to do whatever it takes to rebuild trust as quickly as possible by taking responsibility for your mistakes. If you are the person who has been hurt, again, you should not be over-dramatic or make it hard for the other side, thereby giving him or her the opportunity to say, "I have tried and I do not know what else I can do. So be it. Let the house be destroyed! What can I do?" Do not make it difficult for the other person. We pray in Divine Liturgy, "Straighten for us the way of godliness" (Divine Liturgy according to St. Gregory). Therefore, each of the two sides has a role. Remember that we have all caused problems in our lives, and we go to our fathers of confession and confess to God. Then, Abouna tells us that God has forgiven us, and we receive absolution. God does not repay us back as we may think. That is what made King David say, "Let us fall into the hand of the Lord, for His mercies

---

9   Sayedna (Arabic word) is in reference to addressing the pope, a metropolitan, or a bishop.

are great; but do not let me fall into the hand of man" (2 Sam 24:14).

[Please refer to Chapter 4 for more on trust.]

Seven Steps in Forgiveness and Reconciliation

If one of you is hurt by the other, what can you do?

1. Schedule a meeting to discuss the issue. Schedule it for an appropriate time and in an appropriate place. For example, this meeting should not take place while one spouse is getting ready for work or the other is rushing to take the children to school. You cannot discuss an important issue while both of you are under stress, trying to get where you need to go. Sometimes, when I am leaving a meeting and the place is crowded and people are trying to greet me, one person chooses this moment to ask me about a problem that is extremely important in his life. If the problem is that important to you, do not ask for my opinion while I am walking out of a crowded meeting and things are stressful. It does not work that way. Therefore, choose the right place and time. I know that there is something irritating you, making you want to discuss the issue because you are upset and hurt and cannot wait. However, if you want the discussion to be effective, choose the right time and place.

    Of course, the other person may tell you, "Now is not the right time!" When you ask when the right time would be, the answer is always, "later." "Later" never comes! Therefore, the other person must give an exact time he or she thinks is most conducive. We cannot just say, "later." A date or an appointment is acceptable, but *later* is unacceptable. Both spouses should be calm and agree on a time when both are spiritually and psychologically ready for a discussion.

2. Start this meeting with prayer; then, discuss the issue. Do not discuss the past and everything that happened before the last incident; this will overwhelm the other person. When you try to discuss twenty topics in the same sitting, it simply will not work. You are here for this particular topic, so discuss this

topic only. If, during the discussion, old reasons come up that need to be discussed, mention them briefly.

Some couples talk to me about their entire history and every problem they have had from the time they were engaged. By the time we reach today's problem, I am already falling asleep! This is not going to work. Do not overwhelm the other person with the problems. Identify the problem or the harmful event and talk about it.

3. Explore the pain and concern related to the issue from both sides. Each one of you has a point of view; listen to each other and do not belittle, underestimate, or ignore the other person's pain and feelings. Listen carefully and understand the other person's pain.

    When you talk, do not attack because this will bring forth opposite results and make the other person defensive. There is a difference between saying, "I was hurt by that comment," vs. "You hurt me!" "You hurt me" means "You meant to hurt me." However, perhaps I got hurt but you did not mean to hurt me. When you use the word "you," this is an attack because it indicates that the other person did something. On the other hand, "I" statements indicate my own feelings. Therefore, use "I" statements instead of "You" statements.

4. The person at fault must ask for forgiveness, even if the mistake was unintentional, as we explained.

5. The offended person should offer genuine forgiveness, from the heart, and not hypocritically. Also, the offended person should make the other person's repentance easy and not dramatize the situation. Remember that forgiveness is unconditional while reconciliation is conditional.

6. The person at fault should make positive comments about changing the attitude or pattern that hurts the other person.

He should do this personally, without encouragement from the other person, as part of taking responsibility for his mistakes. He or she can say, "As for me, I will do [or not do] such and such because I know that this upsets you." This is much better than when the person who was hurt says, "Here is my list of conditions." In this case, each side would be setting conditions for the other. On the other hand, when the person at fault shows serious and genuine responsibility on his own, this can help quickly rebuild trust.

7. Expect healing to take time. Any wound takes time to heal. At the end, restoration and reconciliation will take place, and we will live together in peace.

If spouses apply these seven points when we feel that they had wronged each other, there will truly be peace and love between them and they will be able to live peaceably with each other. As I told you, we all hurt each other and all of us have been hurt. That is why forgiveness and reconciliation are components life that we cannot live without them.

May God give us forgiveness for one another and lives of peace and love, as the Holy Bible says, "Blessed are the peacemakers, for they shall be called sons of God" (Mt 5:9).

Part III
THE CHRISTIAN FAMILY

CHAPTER

CHAPTER
10 Holiness in the Family (Homily to Youth)

Challenges to the Life of Holiness and How to Ovecome Them

  Culture

  Accept and Expect Differentness

  Present Your Standards Clearly

  Arm Yourself

  Be Proactive

  Be Separate

  Television

  Computers and the Internet

  Curfew

Contributing to the Life of Holiness in the Family

  The Family Altar

  Respect and Honor Your Parents

  Keep Christian Values

  Contribute to Household Chores

  The Life of Discipleship in the Family

  Be Active Members in the Church

"Holiness" can be defined in two words: *Jesus Christ*, and being *Christ-like*. All of us are required to be Christ-like in our lives. That is the standard God expects, and He does not accept anything lower. Regarding this, St. Paul uses the phrase, "The fullness of Christ" (Eph 4:13). We need to set the standard in order to know toward what we are working and how much effort is needed.

If we define a holy life as being Christ-like, then a holy family is *church-like*. In my life, I should be Christ-like, and my house should be church-like. When I enter your house and visit your family, it is as if I am visiting a church. That is why, in the letters of St. Paul, we read this verse several times: "Greet the church in their house" (see Rom 16:5, 1 Cor 16:19, Col 4:15, and Philem 1:2). The houses of believers are churches. How can youth and children contribute to the life of holiness in their families? There is a positive way to contribute, meaning there are things we need to do, and there is contribution in a negative sense, meaning things we need to avoid. The second question is: What are the challenges to living the life of holiness in your family, and how can you overcome these challenges?

Challenges to the Life of Holiness and How to Overcome Them

Culture

Let us start with the challenges. The first challenge is culture. This challenge exists in daily life, and may be reflected in families. We live in an American society in which the standard is different from that of Christianity. This is not only true regarding American society, but also Egyptian society. The standard of the world is different than the standard of the Church. The Lord Jesus Christ plainly said, "You are not of this world" (Jn 15:19), and St. Paul said, "Do not be conformed to this world" (Rom 12:2). These verses mean that the world's standards are different from the Church's standard of being Christ-like.

Accept and Expect Differentness

How can we face this challenge? First, you need to *accept* that you are different. The problem is that many of us do not accept this challenge. We do not want to be different. This is why it is easier for us to be conformed to the world rather than to be transformed. We do not want to be against the world, so we yield to pressure and conform. In our hearts, we do not accept this challenge. If we accepted it, I think we would be fine with it. However, I hear many youth say, "We do not want to be different" or, "Why should I be different?" To be Christian, you must be different, not in a bad way, but in a better way. In other words, it is not about being different, but about being unique. Once we accept and expect this, and we expect that others will perceive us as different, I think we will be able to handle it and deal with it.

Present Your Standards Clearly

The second piece of advice is that you need to clearly present your Christian values and morals to everybody. You need to live up to your standards and say, "I am Christian." For example, if they ask you why you do not have a girlfriend or a boyfriend, the answer is not, "Because I do not want to have a mate now," or "I am busy with my studies." This hides your Christianity as if you are doing something bad. What is amazing is that the children of the world brag about their standards, and sometimes we feel embarrassed and want to hide the goodness and the virtue in us. I do not want you to brag pridefully in a sinful way, but you can say very clearly, "I do not date because I am Christian." That is it. That is my standard. I do not drink because I am Christian. I do not go to parties because I am Christian. I do not smoke, and I do not do drugs because I am Christian. I cannot participate with you in this discussion because I am Christian. This is my standard and I will not compromise it, period. I will not negotiate. I will not argue about it.

We should not negotiate. If a thief came to your house and knocked at the door, you would not negotiate with him and say, "No, you cannot come in now; you cannot steal my money at this time." Sometimes we negotiate with sin. The devil is the thief that comes to steal your purity, your chastity, and, sometimes, you negotiate with him. "Okay, can we do this but not that? What are the limits and the boundaries? When is it right and when is it wrong?" Negotiating is the first step toward sin. Do not negotiate.

Arm Yourself

You need to arm yourself with weapons. You are expecting external attacks from the devil, so do not go into the world spiritually unarmed. You need to prepare yourself and be ready for these assaults. For example, peer pressure is a strike from the devil and the world. The best way to prepare yourself is with the Word of God. David said, "Your word I have hidden in my heart, that I might not sin against You" (Ps 119:11). If we hide the word of God and keep it in our hearts, like St. Mary (see Lk 2:19, 51), when we are attacked, we can respond by the word: "It is written…" In the temptation on the mountain, our Lord Jesus Christ responded to the devil's attacks with verses from the Holy Scripture. Thus, you need to arm yourself with the word of God.

Be Proactive

My fourth piece of advice to you is to be proactive. Do not simply wait for an attack and then defend yourself, but be assertive and take initiative to witness to the Lord Jesus Christ. Instead of waiting until they speak about something you do not want to hear and then telling them, "No, I do not want to hear about this because I am Christian, and it is written…," initiate discussions about Christ, righteousness, purity, chastity, the Holy Spirit, and the sanctification and consecration of life. Lead these types of discussions. St. Paul initiated a conversation with Felix the governor in which he spoke with him about chastity, righteousness, and the Day of Judgment (see Act 24:24–26). It is true that Felix did not listen to him, and that is fine, but St. Paul did his part. Do your part regardless of whether or not they listen.

Be Separate

You need to separate yourself from the world. Be separate. If there is a place that does not glorify God, you should not be there. I am not speaking about situations that you cannot avoid. You cannot avoid walking down the street and seeing or hearing something offensive. In these situations, you need to use the word of God as your weapon. However, there are many other situations that you can avoid. If you are not there, there will be no pressure. Once you are there, there will be pressure; so, avoid being there. Do not be in places or with people that create pressure.

The Greek word for *church*, "ekikliseya," can be broken into two parts: "ek" means *outside* and "kliseya" means *assemble*. Therefore, "ekikliseya" means *assemble outside to meet with the Lord*. To be a church means to separate yourself, to isolate yourself, from the world to meet with God, to assemble with Christ. It is separation from the world to be united with the Lord. That is the exact meaning of the word *church*.

Television

Television is a second challenge to the life of holiness in the family. It sets an unrealistic example and it can brainwash viewers. For example, when you watch movies in which dating is considered normal, you will think that it is normal to have a boyfriend or girlfriend. A second example is violence. Sometimes, many problems in movies are solved using violence, and the person who carries a gun is presented as a hero; you may sympathize with him or her. The movie justifies this person's actions, to the extent that you believe that what he is doing is right. Thus, the problem with television is more than just bad language. Ideas and teachings are presented in a way that can desensitize you or make you sympathize with them.

Nowadays, families in which both parents work, sometimes the real parent is the TV, and not the father or the mother. Both of them are very busy with their lives and work, and when they get home, they are extremely exhausted and do not have time to spend with their children or communicate with them. However, the TV is on for hours every day. The TV has become a parent to many children. The TV is the one teaching your family morals and values, and this is a real danger to the holiness of the family (not to mention all the profanity, sexual innuendos, and violence).

Think about how many hours you watch TV and how many hours you pray and attend church. Many complain that the liturgy is too long. If I take an average right now of how many hours of TV you watch, I am sure that most of you watch more than four hours a week. You watch more than four hours of TV a week, yet do you not accept to pray for four hours in the Divine Liturgy? How many hours every day do you watch TV and how many hours do you pray and read the Holy Bible? Examine yourself and answer this question honestly.

Moreover, when you watch TV, you are a passive learner. You sit down and relax, and the TV puts information into your mind. You do not use your mind or do anything. Many researchers have found that the intelligence and IQ level of a person who watches TV for four hours every day may decrease, since this person is not using his mind. You do not exercise the ability to think on your own. For example, for those who are right-handed, their left hand is weaker than their right hand because they do not use it. For left-handed people, their right hand is weaker because they do not use it. If you do not use your brain, it will stop thinking. If your brain stops thinking, your IQ will go down.

For example, because Egyptian physicians do not have the same kind of equipment and facilities that American physicians have, they use their intelligence. In fact, in medical school in Egypt, they taught us how to diagnose a patient from the way he looks, the color of his face, the color of his nails, and the way he walks. Egyptian physicians are very talented in diagnosing without X-rays or anything like that. However, it is different here because everything is done using CAT scans, X-rays, blood analysis, etc. Unless the CAT scan says that this is what you have, there is nothing wrong with you, even if you are complaining. Furthermore, since accounting is now done solely using computers and calculators, most of us do not know how to calculate using our minds. My father worked in accounting, and he used to add, multiply, and subtract big numbers in his head. I was amazed. This is what it means to use the mind. If you do not use it, your IQ level will decrease. The same applies to TV: Being a passive receiver of information for four hours every day will lower your IQ. TV is a real challenge and a threat to the life of holiness in the family. Of course, TV, like anything, can be used in a constructive or destructive way. There are many good ways to use TV.

Computers and the Internet

Even if you are using the Internet in the right way by not visiting inappropriate websites, it is a threat to the life of holiness if you abuse it by spending too many hours on your computer. It is now well known that computers are addictive, like drugs. People get treated for computer and Internet addiction. The second point is that the Internet and computers separate you from the family. You sit inside your room, by yourself, doing whatever it is that you are doing. Physically, you are in the house, but, in reality, you are not. A person can spend hours on the computer without realizing it; therefore, you need to manage your time. This is a warning about computer and Internet addiction and how it takes you away from family.

Curfew

Another challenge is curfew. Staying out late is not good. When I was your age, in high school or college, I used to go to quiet areas in Cairo with my friends for meditation and we would do spiritual things. For example, during the week each of us would read certain chapters from the Holy Bible; then, we would meet at church every Thursday and pray the Vespers Hour together. Then, we would go somewhere quiet, such as the Cathedral, to spend some time in a peaceful atmosphere, meditating, talking, and reflecting about what we had read during the past week. We concluded with prayer and we would go back to the church to pray the Midnight Hour together. Then, we would go home. We used to do this every week. One night, we were in the cathedral at about 10:00 p.m., and Bishop Timothy saw both of us walking around. He asked us what we were doing there so late. We explained what we were doing, which was 100% spiritual. He told us, "I do not agree with this. As youth, you should be home early, because if you are here until 10:00, when you get home, it will be 11:00 or 11:30, and you will not have enough time to pray, read the Holy Bible, and sleep early enough to get up early for the liturgy." We had liturgy every Friday in Egypt. Although we were doing a spiritual activity, he did not encourage us at all. We learned a lesson and we did not argue with him. We were obedient, listened to his advice, and we agreed to finish the meeting every Thursday at 8:00 in order to arrive home by 8:30.

I confess, at first, I obeyed him and listened to him, but I was not convinced, because I felt I was doing something spiritual. However, we grew up accustomed to always obeying bishops and priests without discussion, and that is why we obeyed him. *After* we obeyed him, we learned and benefitted from the experience itself, and we realized that his advice was correct.

When I discuss curfew, I am not talking about unavoidable situations, such as work, for example. If you are a physician and they call you in at midnight, you cannot say, "I am sorry; my curfew is at 10:00." However, if you have a choice to take the day shift, that is much better. I am speaking about when it is your choice, and this is for children, youth, *and* adults. When you are home early, go to sleep early, and wake up early; this is healthier.

Contributing to the Life of Holiness in the Family

How can youth contribute to the life of holiness in the family?

The Family Altar

As a member in your family, you should participate with the rest of your family in gathering and assembling around the family altar, praying together, reading the Holy Bible together, and fasting together. I know many youth do not fast, but their parents fast. There is no good explanation for this. I am aware that in some houses, it is the other way around, but I am speaking about the majority of situations. I do not know why youth do not fast. Or, sometimes they fast at home, but once they leave the house, they stop at the first restaurant they see to get a burger.

Fast together, pray together, and read the Holy Bible together. I hope you have a day in which the whole family goes to church and takes communion together; every member of the family takes communion on the same day. This is what we call the family altar. As a member in the family, you should contribute to this. Sometimes, parents complain that their children do not want to participate or share in this time. When they ask them to join them in reading the Holy Bible, they respond by saying that they are too busy and that they will read it later. This is not right. You need to read the Holy Bible by yourself and also with your family. Family unity is the oneness of the family, and nothing will keep you united except God and the family altar. You need to gather around the family altar together. By doing this, you will keep the unity and oneness of the family.

Do not be a trouble-maker in your family. Do not be a source of conflict, but be a peacemaker. You cause peace to be lost in the family. When teenagers are disobedient and argue with their parents, sometimes they upset everybody. One disobedient teenager can upset everyone in the family. The Christian life is a life of sacrifice; even if you sacrifice your own rights, or something that you believe is 100% right, keeping the peace and the holiness of the family is much better. For example, a major argument can start because of curfew. Which is better: To be obedient and go home early, keep the curfew and the peace of the family, and make everybody happy (even if this is unfair to you), or to insist on what you want and start a fight? Christianity means sacrifice—to sacrifice oneself. The Lord died on the cross and showed His love by sacrificing Himself. You should not ask, "Why me? Why don't *they* sacrifice?" You are Christian, and every Christian should live the life of sacrifice. Obedience is a very good way to keep the holiness in the family. I can tell how much parents suffer when they have a disobedient child.

Respect and Honor Your Parents

Respecting and honoring our parents are ways to keep the holiness in the family. Sometimes, we do not know how to treat our parents with honor and respect. His Holiness Pope Shenouda III of thrice blessed memory wrote a book about honoring parents, and I recommend that everyone reads it. One of the stories that His Holiness mentioned in the book is about how his older brother took care of him because their mother departed very shortly after the birth of His Holiness and their father departed when His Holiness was a child. His older brother became a father to him, and simply because he took care of him, His Holiness said that he never called his brother by his name. He felt that it would have been disrespectful to do so. His brother's name was Raphael, and he could not address him as "Raphael." This is the extent to which he respected his older brother, simply because he took care of him. How many times do we deal with our parents in a disrespectful way?

When King Solomon's mother came in to meet with him, he rose up to meet her, bowed to her, and set a throne for her next to his (see 1 Kg 2:19). He was a king. It is the same with our Lord Jesus Christ. He respected His mother when she asked him to do a miracle and help the people of Cana in Galilee, although His hour had not yet come. One of my favorite verses about the Lord is in the Gospel of Luke: "Then He went down with them and came to Nazareth, and was subject to them" (Lk 2:51–52). He was submissive to His parents; He is the Lord, their *Creator*, but now, because He is their Child, He was obedient to them. When we become obedient and understand how to deal with our parents respectfully, we will keep the life of holiness in our families.

[Please refer to Chapter 14 for more on honoring parents.]

Keep Christian Values

We need to keep Christian values in our families. We must make our families Christian. We need to live up to this standard, and be Christ-like and church-like. When you enter the house, you must feel that you are in a church. When I enter some houses, I do not find any icons, but rather many pictures of cars, singers, and athletes. In your own room, you need to have an icon of the Lord Jesus Christ, an icon of St. Mary, and an icon of your patron saint. You need to have your own Bible and Agpeya. You need to have Christian media in your house. Sometimes, if I look at your CDs, it is very hard to find a single Christian CD. I find many CDs that are non-Christian. What are you listening to? If you are listening to non-Christian music all day, you are not using music to contribute to the life of holiness in the family. This is not a church. I expect to hear Christian songs in a church, not rock or rap music. I am not expecting this at all.

Have a Christian library. How many Christian books do you have, other than the Holy Bible? What do you read? Every church should have a library, and your house, as a church, should have a Christian library. You should start collecting Christian books and have them available, and you should read these books.

Contribute to Household Chores

You need to contribute to whatever work is done in the house. When you work in your house and serve, you will feel like you belong. This feeling of belonging strengthens the ties between the family members. Sometimes, we live as strangers in our houses, and if we do something, we ask our parents to give us money or an allowance in return. "I cut the grass; how much are you going to give me?" This is not right. You cannot do this. You are not a hireling. You are a son or a daughter in this house. It is your house. You are not a maid. Also, you cannot simply watch your parents as they work. That is not Christian.

The Life of Discipleship in the Family

We need to understand the boundaries and sub-systems of the family. We need to understand the role of the parents and the role of the children. Sometimes, we invert the hierarchy and lecture our parents, as if we know better. No. You need to understand the order and hierarchy in the family. God asked children to obey and honor their parents. He gave another commandment to the parents about not aggravating their children. That is their role, but you, as children, need to be obedient. You need to be obedient, not until you get married, but your entire life.

<u>Be Active Members in the Church</u>

The last point is church life. We do not want to be strangers in our church. Sometimes, we simply attend church, but we are not active in the life of the church. You should participate in all the activities in the church as a family. I do not like seeing just some members of the family are in church while others are not. I do not want you to be the absent member. If you do not have control over others, you should at least be present at church activities. I do not expect your parents to go to church for Vespers, and you go out with your friends, for example. This is not right. As a family, you go together to be active in church life. If you are active in church life, you will take this church with you in your homes, and your houses will be converted into churches.

To summarize, you should be Christ-like in your life, and your houses should be church-like. If you forget everything that we discussed, remember these two words, "Christ-like" and "church-like;" that is fine. Be Christ-like and make your house church-like. It is very simple.

11 The Role of the Holy Bible in the Family

The Holy Bible

Relevance of the Holy Bible

The Holy Bible is Profitable for Teaching

The Holy Bible is Profitable for Reproof

The Holy Bible is Profitable for Correction

The Holy Bible is Profitable for Training

The Holy Bible Communicates God's Voice

The Holy Bible Sets the Standard for Our Lives

The Holy Bible Changes Us

When we remind ourselves of God's teachings on family principles, this will not only enrich our family relationships, but also strengthen our church, enabling us to be strong witnesses to the Lord Jesus Christ in the society in which we live.

The Holy Bible

The Holy Bible is like a manual. Whenever you buy a new computer or any other machine, it comes with a manual, which teaches you how to use the machine effectively. In it, there are instructions as well as warnings. When you follow the instructions and try to avoid the warnings, you will be able to use the machine effectively. In the same way, God is our Creator, our Manufacturer. He gave us *this* Manual, the Holy Bible, which has instructions on how to deal with each other as well as warnings about things we should avoid in order to live happy and godly lives. The Holy Bible, as a Manual, has instructions concerning marriage, family relationships, parenting, family conflicts, intimacy, and all other aspects of family life. Thus, the Holy Bible is not only a book that teaches us how to live a godly life and go to heaven, but it also has clear instructions concerning all the details of family life.

As with any manual, you need to read it carefully to understand the instructions. You also need to memorize it, share it with others, and apply it. Thus, in order to benefit from the Holy Bible in our lives, we need to read it carefully, understand what we read, and memorize it, as David the Prophet says, "Your word I have hidden in my heart, that I might not sin against You" (Ps 119:11)." We also need to share it, as is explained in Deuteronomy 6:6. In this verse, there are clear instructions from God about sharing the word of God with your children and family. You also need to apply it in your life. If you do this, you will have a happy family, but if you do not do this, you will have a dysfunctional family.

The Holy Bible is our guide to life and having a happy family. That is why I would like to start by giving you an idea of what the Holy Bible is. The Holy Bible is a collection of 76 different books divided into two sections, the Old Testament and the New Testament. The Old Testament is composed of 49 books. If you have a Protestant version of the Holy Bible, there will only be 39 books in the Old Testament. However, the Orthodox Bible has 49 books in the Old Testament, according to the Septuagint translation, which is the oldest translation of the Old Testament. The Lord Jesus Christ Himself, as well as the apostles and all the early Church Fathers, used and quoted the Septuagint translation. The New Testament is composed of 27 books.

The Holy Bible was written by over 40 different authors. They were different in all aspects. We have kings (David), farmers (Amos), fishermen (St. Peter), and physicians (Luke), differing in education and occupations. It was written over a period of 1,500 years, 15 centuries, and in three different languages. The New Testament was mostly in Greek, and the Old Testament mostly in Hebrew, with some Aramaic. Although the Holy Bible was written by over 40 different authors over a span of 15 centuries, it presents a unified message. When you read the Holy Bible, you will feel that there is harmony. There is no difference between the Old Testament and the New Testament. There are no contradictions in the Holy Bible. You sense the harmony in presenting God's plan toward humanity.

The Holy Bible was written between 1500 BC and 100 AD. The first book that was written in the Holy Bible is not the Book of Genesis, but the Book of Job. The last book was the Revelation of Jesus Christ. The Holy Bible contains history, poetry, prophecy, letters, biographies, psalms, journals, advice, laws, and stories. Thus, it is not only a book that teaches us how to live a godly life and go to heaven, although that is the main message, but it also includes all these different things. Finally, the entire Bible has been translated into 670 languages, and the New Testament has been translated into 1,521 different languages.

Relevance of the Holy Bible

The Holy Bible is extremely relevant to our lives. What do I mean by this? In 2 Timothy 3:16, St. Paul says to his disciple, Timothy: "All scripture is inspired by God and profitable for teaching, for reproof, for correction, and for training in righteousness" (RSV). Here, St. Paul is emphasizing more than one fact. The first fact is that the Holy

Bible is sacred writing, because the word "Scripture" means *sacred writing*. We call the Holy Bible, "Scripture," or sacred writing, because it is inspired by God. It is God who speaks in the Holy Bible; it is the word of God. It is the voice of God. Every word in the Holy Bible is inspired by God. That is why the Holy Bible, as a Manual, is profitable for four things: teaching, reproof, correction, and training in righteousness.

The fundamental characteristic of Scripture, what makes this writing sacred, is the fact that God breathed it out. The word "inspired" means *breathed out*, and that its ultimate origin is with God Himself. It is God who is the real Author of the Holy Bible, and that is why the Holy Bible has vital, practical relevance to our lives. St. Paul says, this relevance is seen in four areas. We are going to apply these four areas to family life in the next section.

The Holy Bible is Profitable for Teaching

The Holy Bible is a teacher for the family. The word "teaching" focuses on how the Holy Bible gives us instructions on how to live. If the Holy Bible is a teacher, we have to approach it in the spirit of a student. Some people do not regard the Holy Bible in this way, and that is why they do not benefit from it. They may read the Holy Bible in order to criticize it. As long as you do not read the Holy Bible in the spirit of learning, you will not benefit from it. St. Augustine shared this fact with us. At first, he read the Holy Bible in order to criticize it and prove that it is false, and that is why he did not learn anything. However, when he started reading in order to learn, it transformed his life.

The instruction, or teaching, in the Holy Bible is not only about heavenly things but also addresses practical points in our lives and our families, such as how to be a good spouse, how to be a good parent, and how to resolve our conflicts.

The Holy Bible is Profitable for Reproof

The second area is reproof. Reproof means confronting our wrong ideas about life and God. Each one of us may have some incorrect beliefs or ideas. Every person has a belief system, which is the set of beliefs you have about life, yourself, and God. Some of these beliefs, or ideas, are wrong. It is the Holy Bible that confronts our wrong ideas about God. For example, sometimes, parents give their children wrong ideas about God. A mother may constantly tell her son: "If you do this, God will be angry with you." This child will believe that God is easily angered. A child once said to his mother: "I think God is angry with me all the time. What can I do to please Him?" Because his mother's comments were unwise, her son developed a wrong perception about God, that He is angry all the time. However, when the child starts reading the Holy Bible, for example, in Jonah 4 about how God is slow to anger, then the Holy Bible will confront and challenge these wrong ideas about God. In this way, the Holy Bible reproofs him, transforms him, and gives him the correct idea about God.

This assumes that all of us sometimes have misconceptions and distortions about God, family, life, and ourselves. When we read the Holy Bible regularly, these wrong ideas will be corrected, because these beliefs need to be changed. For example, someone may believe that the measure of a good spouse is how much money a person has; a young woman presented with multiple suitors may believe that a good spouse is someone who provides well for his family. However, when she starts reading the Holy Bible, it will teach her that a good spouse is a person who is faithful to God, not the person who makes much money. The Holy Bible reproved her ideas and beliefs, about a good spouse, and she will start to change her belief system in order to conform to God's definition.

The Holy Bible is Profitable for Correction

The Holy Bible is also profitable for correction. While reproof targets the belief system—your ideas, beliefs, conceptions, and perceptions—correction focuses on behavior; it addresses how to correct behavior. The Holy Bible will help you correct your behavior when you start to drift away. All of us, at certain moments in our lives, may lose the right way. We may drift away from the true way to eternal life and wander off the course that God has set for us. The Holy Bible will correct our behaviors and bring us back to the true way. For example, if a husband holds a grudge against his wife, but he starts reading the Holy Bible, it will correct this behavior and teach him how to forgive. The Holy Bible will do this through examples, such as our Lord Jesus Christ or St. Stephen, and also through many commandments, such as those in the writings of St. Paul or St. Peter. Thus, the teachings about forgiveness will correct wrong behavior. Instead of behaving in an angry way toward one's spouse, the Holy Bible will make him a forgiving person and give him the spirit of forgiveness.

The Holy Bible shows us where we are currently and how to get back on track. That is why St. James says that the Holy Bible is like a mirror (see Jas 1:23–25). In the same way that you see yourself in a mirror, the Holy Bible is your spiritual mirror. When you read it, it will tell you where you are spiritually. Not only will it tell you where you are spiritually, it will also tell you how to correct your way and return to God.

The Holy Bible is Profitable for Training

In school, there are both lectures and labs. In lab, you receive training in what you learned in the lectures. As St. Paul said, the Holy Bible is also good for training in righteousness. The Holy Bible teaches us and helps us live a life that pleases God, a life that God wants us to live. This implies that it is not merely reading the Holy Bible that will transform you and change your life. A life of integrity, perfection, and holiness does not come naturally to us. You need to train yourself in order to live the life of integrity that God wants you to live, and the Holy Bible is what will train you. It trains us to do that which we could not do on our own when it comes to a life of integrity. You cannot live a life of perfection and holiness or have a happy family without this specific kind of training.

Therefore, the Holy Bible is relevant in our lives because it is inspired by God—God is the author of the Bible—and it is profitable for teaching, reproof, correction, and training in righteousness.

The Holy Bible Communicates God's Voice

People often ask how they can know or recognize God's voice, and how they can know His will for them. The Holy Bible is the voice of God to you: "Knowing this first, that no prophecy of Scripture is of any private interpretation, for prophecy never came by the will of man, but holy men of God spoke as they were moved by the Holy Spirit" (2 Pet 1:20–21). Here, St. Peter uses the word "prophecy" in reference to the Holy Bible and, as we discussed, St. Paul uses the word "Scripture" to refer to the Bible. What does St. Peter mean by the word, "prophecy?" Prophesying does not simply mean to predict or foretell future events, as commonly thought. The word "prophecy" refers to how God reveals things that we could not figure out on our own. When we say the Holy Bible is the prophecy of God, this means that the Bible is the book that contains God's revelations. God reveals Himself in the Holy Bible. We can recognize His words in the Bible. Part of this revelation is prediction, so future events could prove that this revelation is true. However, the focus of prophecy is God revealing Himself. Therefore, when St. Peter says that no prophecy of Scripture is of private interpretation, he is not speaking about foretelling the future. He is speaking about God revealing Himself to humanity.

There are also two points in these verses that I want to discuss: the phrase "private interpretation" and the word "moved." When St. Peter says, "Knowing this first, that no prophecy of Scripture is of any private interpretation," he is saying very clearly that the Holy Bible is not a matter of the reader's or the author's own interpretation. The human authors of the Holy Bible did not put their own interpretations into the Bible, and neither should the readers. If no prophecy came through private interpretation, this means that private interpretation of both the author and the reader is prohibited. Through the inspiration of the Holy Spirit, God protected the authors of the Holy Bible from inserting their own private interpretations. That is why when we interpret the Holy Bible as readers, we should yield and submit to the meaning that God intended by His word, not the meaning that we like or prefer.

There are hundreds of denominations in the world that call themselves Christians and use the same Bible. However, there are big differences amongst these denominations. These differences are not found in the text of the Bible, but in the interpretation. It is a big problem when we interpret the Holy Bible according to our own understanding. That is why many people have deviated from the truth in the Holy Bible. Although they use the Bible, they interpret it according to their own understanding. That is why St. Peter warned us against private interpretation. We cannot make the Holy Bible say whatever we want it to say. Therefore, this verse is warning us not to force our own interpretation.

Whenever we try to use our own interpretation of the Holy Bible, we put ourselves in danger of missing God's voice but hearing our own voice instead of His. That is why the Holy Bible will not help you or benefit you in this case because you are reading your own ideas, and hearing your own voice. That is why St. Peter said that the holy men of God wrote the Holy Bible *moved* by the Holy Spirit, which means it is God who initiated the process of writing the Holy Scripture and giving us the Holy Bible, not the human authors. We should understand that the human authors used their own style of writing, but God spoke through them. The concept of inspiration in Christianity is completely different from the concept of inspiration in Islam. In Islamic inspiration, according to their belief, somebody dictated the Quran to the prophet. Therefore, inspiration in Islam is a process of dictation. However, in Christianity, the authors were moved by the Holy Spirit, but they kept their own writing styles. They were not robots, but each one kept his own method, and God protected them from inserting their own private interpretations. That is the work of the Holy Spirit in inspiration.

The human authors of the Holy Bible were consciously involved in the writing process; we can even detect their own unique writing styles and differentiate between them. Ultimately, every word in the Holy Bible is inspired by the Holy Spirit and God is the one who moved the authors to write. Behind the writing process, the Holy Spirit was moving them to ensure that the end result would be *exactly* what God wanted to say, not what they wanted to say. That is why St. Peter emphasizes the point that private interpretation was not present.

The Holy Bible Sets the Standard for our Lives

The Holy Bible sets the standard for our lives. If it sets a standard for our lives, in general, then it also sets the standards for family life. For example, the Holy Bible is against polygamy, so this is a standard. The Lord Jesus Christ said, "He who made them at the beginning made them male and female" (Mt 19:4). He did not create a male and *females* (if He had wanted polygamous societies), but He created one male and one female. Another example is that the Holy Bible teaches that homosexuality is a sin, and we cannot consider homosexuals a family. There are some notions now that a family can be defined as two people living together, even if they are the same gender. No. The Holy Bible said that from the beginning, God created them male and female. Another standard is divorce. The Lord Jesus Christ says very clearly that the intention of God is for the wife not to leave her husband and for the husband not to leave his wife. Thus, there are standards and specific directives in the Holy Bible for the family.

We read in John 17:17 that the Lord Jesus Christ says, "Sanctify them by Your truth. Your word is truth." If His word is truth, we can replace the word "truth" with the word, "word," and say, "Sanctify them by Your word." What exactly is truth? Truth is whatever corresponds to facts; something that matches the way things really are is true. When we say, "This statement is a truthful statement," this means, "This statement corresponds to reality." The Holy Bible, the word of God, corresponds to the reality of our lives, because it is true. A key characteristic of the Holy Bible, as the Lord Jesus Christ said in John 17:17, is its truthfulness. "Your word is truth." If God is the origin of the Holy Bible and if God is truthful, the Holy Bible *must* be true. In other words, the Holy Bible is truthful because it is the word of God, and God is true.

By saying that the Holy Bible is truthful, we are saying that the Bible tells us the way things really are, and that it accurately describes reality. Thus, the Holy Bible's description about family is the reality about family. When the Holy Bible says that the family should be one male and one female, and there is no polygamy, this is truth, and this is the reality about the family. When the Holy Bible says that it is one male and one female, not two males or two females, this is another reality about the family. When the Holy Bible says that God hates divorce, and there is no divorce except in the case of adultery, this is another reality about the family. That is how the family should be, and that is how the Holy Bible accurately describes the family. What the Holy Bible teaches about sex is the reality about sex. You cannot insert your own interpretation. The world tries to condone sex outside the boundaries of marriage, but the Holy Bible does not teach this; thus, this nonbiblical publicity contradicts reality. You can only find reality in the Holy Bible.

We should not put our own interpretations about the family into the Holy Bible, because we will fail to hear God's voice and message to us. We should learn from the Holy Bible, as our teacher, because the Bible is profitable for teaching. We should learn the standards that the Bible sets for our lives, especially for our families. This makes the Holy Bible a comprehensive and conclusive, Christian standard for what is true.

Thus far we have covered three points: The Holy Bible is relevant to our lives, communicates the voice of God, and sets the standards, especially family standards, for our lives.

The Holy Bible Changes Us

The last point is that the Holy Bible changes and transforms us. In Hebrews 4:12, St. Paul says, "For the word of God is living and powerful, and sharper than any two-edged sword, piercing even to the division of soul and spirit, and of joints and marrow, and is a discerner of the thoughts and intents of the heart." Here, there is another description of the Holy Bible; so, far we spoke of the Bible as Scripture, or sacred writing, as prophecy, or as God revealing Himself, and now, it is described as the word of God. When we say that the word of God is living and active, we are referring to a dynamic element. When you read the word of God, because it is living and active, it can transform and change you. Therefore, the word of God not only educates you, but also has the power to transform you. That is why St. Paul said that it is sharper than a two-edged sword.

The word of God will pierce deep into your heart, soul, spirit, joints, and marrow. The soul is the center of desires, so the word of God pierces into the soul to sanctify your desires. The spirit is the center of the mind and thought. The difference between animals and human beings is the spirit, which gives human beings the ability to think. When the word of God pierces into your spirit, it sanctifies your thoughts. Joints are for movement, so the word of God pierces into your joints to sanctify your actions and your works, and into the marrow to sanctify your will. Thus, the word of God transforms your desires, thoughts, works, and will. It discerns the thoughts and intentions of the heart. Even if there is something hidden in the innermost soul, the word of God will search and bring it into the light. Why? Because it is living and active. It is sharp. It goes deep inside to your core and destroys the old person and builds and raises the new person in Christ.

Although the Holy Bible reveals God's truth to us, its primary purpose is not merely to educate us, but also to change us—to transform us. This is what makes the Holy Bible different from any other book. Any other book will educate and inform you. However, the Holy Bible does not only inform you, but it also transforms you. It is information and transformation. "The word of God is living and powerful," means that there is a dynamic energy at work when someone reads the Holy Bible. The energy of the word of God, which is active and living, will change you internally. The living God is actively working in and through the words of the Holy Bible to impact and change the reader's life. When you read the Holy Bible as a learner, as a disciple, God Himself, through His word, will change your life and you will be transformed.

The Holy Bible is described as a sharp double-edged sword, which focuses on its ability to penetrate deep into our lives, into our innermost souls. The Holy Bible has no blunt edge, but every part of it is sharp enough to pierce into our lives with its message. We read in the Book of Acts that when the people heard the word of God, "they were cut to the heart" (Acts 2:37). Also, when St. Paul says soul, spirit, joints, and marrow, the focus here is on the Bible's ability to penetrate our defenses, into the very cores of our personalities, where our true selves are. There, at our true selves, at the core of our personalities, the Holy Bible evaluates and discerns our inner thoughts and motives, and filters and sifts through our intentions and ideas by the word that is sharper than a two-edged sword. God works through the Holy Bible to transform us into fully devoted followers of the Lord Jesus Christ and increases our love for God and others.

I want to emphasize that the Christian faith is not merely a set of ideas or beliefs. It is a loving relationship with God. A Christian is not someone who believes in certain ideas, but someone who is in a relationship with God. That is why when John the Baptist saw the Lord Jesus Christ, he described Him as a Bridegroom (see Jn 3:29). He described our relationship with God as a relationship between a Bridegroom and His bride. Christianity is an intimate relationship. This loving relationship is a life-transforming one, because a person cannot encounter the Lord Jesus Christ without being radically and beautifully changed. When St. Paul met the Lord Jesus Christ, his life was fundamentally transformed. Instead of a persecutor, he himself endured persecution for the word of God.

Once we enter this relationship with God, through the Lord Jesus Christ, the Holy Bible becomes one of God's primary means of changing us. It is one of the means of grace, and not the only thing that transforms us. Being a Christian is not merely accepting certain facts about God or about the Holy Bible, but it is becoming a follower and devoted disciple of the Lord Jesus Christ, as we seek to live lives of passionate devotion to Him. The Christian faith is not about being informed and having some ideas and beliefs. It is about being transformed in order to be Christ-like, as St. Paul says, "But we all, with unveiled face, beholding as in a mirror the glory of the Lord, are being transformed into the same image from glory to glory" (2 Cor 3:18).

As I told you, God is not limited to the Holy Bible to transform us; God also transforms us in worship, through the mysteries of the Church (baptism, confession, chrismation, communion), through suffering and carrying His cross, through prayers, through fasting, etc. There are many ways that God is transforming us, but one of the primary ways of transformation is the Holy Bible. The Holy Bible is essential and central to our transformation into the image of

Christ. It is one of the primary means God uses to penetrate past our defenses with this sharp sword to pierce our hearts with His truth so He can sort our thoughts, intentions, and motives.

Some people think that Christianity is just about being informed about God, or reading and studying the Holy Bible. This is not correct. It is more than this. It is a life of transformation, as St. Paul said, "be transformed by the renewing of your mind" (Rom 12:2).

In conclusion, we mentioned four main points about the Holy Bible. First, since God gives us the entire Bible, all its teachings are relevant to our lives. Second, God speaks to us through the Holy Bible, because the Bible communicates the voice of God. Thus, it is important for us to listen to the message of the Bible. God has revealed His truth to us in the Holy Bible, so the Bible is our final standard for what is true. If you want to learn the truth concerning any subject, go to the Holy Bible. Lastly, since God works in our lives through the Holy Bible, it is essential to our spiritual transformation.

12 God Provides for the Family

Relying on God

Relying on God

"Unless the Lord builds the house, they labor in vain who build it; unless the Lord guards the city, the watchman stays awake in vain. It is vain for you to rise up early, to sit up late, to eat the bread of sorrows; for so He gives His beloved sleep. Behold, children are a heritage from the Lord, the fruit of the womb is a reward. Like arrows in the hand of a warrior, so are the children of one's youth. Happy is the man who has his quiver full of them; they shall not be ashamed, but shall speak with their enemies in the gate" (Ps 127).

God provides for the family. "It is vain for you to rise up early, to sit up late, to eat the bread of sorrows; for so He gives His beloved sleep" (Ps 127:2). Holy Scripture certainly does not encourage us to be lazy. I do not want you to misunderstand the verse; it is not speaking about people who work a normal amount, but about people who over-work. They rise up early, they sit up late, and they eat the bread of sorrows. Unfortunately, this is very true in our culture. Many people are workaholics, working day and night. They say that they have a family and need to provide for them. They may work eighteen hours daily to provide their families with a nice house, nice cars, nice clothes— everything. However, they will never provide them with a nice home.

It is very important to spend time with your children. I cannot emphasize this enough. If parents are workaholics and do not give their children time, how will the children be loved, and feel the love and nurture? They will feel abandoned and rejected. They will look for love outside the family. It hurts my heart when I see that there are no longer any family ties or bonds. Family members are like roommates; they do not love each other, because their parents are too busy. We need to trust that God provides for our needs.

I read a very nice story, which I will share with you: A father went to his house after a very long day, and he found his son waiting for him. The son said to his father, "Daddy, how much do you make an hour?" His father looked at him, greatly surprised. Giving his boy a glaring look, his father said, "Look, my son, not even your mother knows that. Do not bother me now, I am tired." His son said, "Daddy, just tell me please—how much do you make an hour?" The boy insisted. The father, finally giving up, replied, "Ten dollars per hour." "Okay, Daddy, could you lend me two dollars?" the boy asked. Angry with his son's constant questions, he said, "Go to sleep and do not bother me anymore!"

It was already dark and the father was feeling guilty for what he said to his son. Maybe his son needed to buy something for school. Finally, wanting to ease his mind, the father went to his son's room. "Are you asleep, son?" asked the father. "No, Daddy, why?" replied the boy, partially sleep. "Here is the money you asked for earlier," the father said. "Thanks Daddy!" rejoiced the son, while putting his hand under his pillow and removing some money. The son said to his father, "Now I have enough. Now I have ten dollars." The father looked at his son, confused by the meaning of what he had said, but the boy continued, "Daddy, can you sell me one hour of your time please?" This story illustrates how much children need to spend time with their parents.

You can provide money for your children, but let me tell you about things that money cannot provide. Money cannot buy love. "But God demonstrates His own love toward us, in that while we were still sinners, Christ died for us" (Rom 5:8). That is the true love; He loves you no matter what. Money cannot buy this kind of love. "A new commandment I give to you, that you love one another; as I have loved you, that you also love one another. By this all will know that you are My disciples, if you have love for one another" (Jn 13:34–35). The Lord says, "As I loved you," so we need to love our children and each other as God loves us.

Money cannot buy acceptance. Our children are often in need of acceptance, especially as middle Eastern immigrants or children of immigrants. Children need to feel accepted. If they feel secure within their homes, they will not look for validation outside the home. St. Paul says, "To the praise of the glory of His grace, by which He made us accepted in the Beloved" (Eph 1:6). God made us accepted in His beloved Son.

Money cannot buy support or encouragement. Yes, you can

provide money for your children, but money cannot give them love, acceptance, support, or encouragement. "And I will pray the Father, and He will give you another Helper, that He may abide with you ... I will not leave you orphans; I will come to you" (Jn 14:16, 18).

Most importantly, money cannot buy forgiveness. I said "most importantly" because all of us are human beings, and all of us make mistakes; no one is without sin. Therefore, in a family, every member will definitely make mistakes. In order to continue as a family, we need to learn how to forgive one another. Without forgiveness, we cannot continue. Why do many couples end up in divorce? It is because they did not learn how to forgive one another. "Be kind to one another, tenderhearted, forgiving one another, even as God in Christ forgave you" (Eph 4:32). We need to forgive one another as Christ forgave us.

It is better to live in a lower socioeconomic level with a healthy, spiritual, and functional family than to live at a very high social level, in a broken family. Those who rise up early, sit up late, and eat the bread of sorrows do so in order to provide more, to live a luxurious life. However, they end up with broken families.

God helps us raise godly children. "Children are a heritage from the Lord, the fruit of the womb is a reward" (Ps 127:3). This is what the Holy Bible teaches about children. Unfortunately, the feminist movement says that children may change the shape of the mother's body, so it is better to adopt than to have children. They also say that women should have control over their bodies, and they can use a surrogate mother. Many fathers feel that children are a burden on their lives. They say that children will make a rich father poor. No. When we die, we will not take anything with us. However, when we go to heaven, if we have raised our children in a godly way, we will take them to God. Therefore, children actually make a poor father *rich*. When he goes to heaven, he will go with many blessed children, and he will say to God, "Here am I and the children whom [You have] given Me ... none of them is lost" (Heb 2:13 and Jn 17:12).

I want you to notice the analogy David uses in the psalm: "Children are a heritage from the Lord, the fruit of the womb is a reward. Like arrows in the hand of a warrior, so are the children of one's youth. Happy is the man who has his quiver full of them; they shall not be ashamed, but shall speak with their enemies in the gate" (Ps 127: 3–5). He says that children are like arrows in the hand of a warrior. When does a warrior have an effect on the arrows—before or after he shoots them? The answer is *before* he shoots them, while they are in his hand. After he shoots the arrows, he does not have control over them. In the same way, the warrior, the father, has an effect on his children while they are still in his hand, before they go into the world and live on their own. While your children are living with you, in your house, from their infancy, that is the best time to start teaching them.

Parenting needs time, effort, teaching, and training. Your children will not grow up just because they are living with you in the house. You need to teach them, raise them, and train them. "Train up a child in the way he should go, and when he is old he will not depart from it" (Prov 22:6). All of this needs time, effort, cost, determination, and patience from you. Without God, we cannot do any of this, because God builds and guards our families, provides for us, and helps us raise godly children.

Part IV
RELATIONSHIPS WITH FAMILY MEMBERS

CHAPTER

13 Winning Over Your Husband

He Who Wins Souls is Wise

Male Psychology

How to Win Over Your Husband

Contention

Revenge and Punishment

Doubt

Jealousy

Contempt and Disrespect

A Crafty Tongue

Overburdening Each Other with Financial Requests

"Wives, likewise, be submissive to your own husbands, that even if some do not obey the word, they, without a word, may be won by the conduct of their wives, when they observe your chaste conduct accompanied by fear" (1 Pet 3:1–2).

He Who Wins Souls is Wise

In these verses (1 Pet 3:1–2), St. Peter talks about a wife's strength in winning over her husband without talking, meaning without preaching. By her chaste conduct, she is able to win over her husband, not to herself, but to Christ. St. Peter is talking about an unusual strength found in women. If her husband is far from God, if he is a man who does not obey the word of God, she has the ability to win him to God without preaching, simply by her conduct. The same idea is mentioned in Proverbs 12:4, "An excellent wife is the crown of her husband".

I want to talk to you about how to win over your husband. The Holy Bible says, "He who wins souls is wise" (Prov 11:30). To be able to win over your husband, you must have wisdom. "The wise woman builds her house" (Prov 14:1). You all know the story of the wise woman, Abigail, whose husband, Nabal, was foolish. With wisdom, Abigail calmed David down when he was angry and determined to kill her husband and everyone in his household. A war was about to start between David and Nabal and their men, but Abigail was able to bring peace, instead of killing and bloodshed. Wisdom is very important in dealing with a husband. Wisdom, in general, is acquired through prayer, as the Holy Bible says, "If any of you lacks wisdom, let him ask of God, who gives to all liberally and without reproach, and it will be given to him" (Jas 1:5). It is also acquired from the Holy Bible itself, "I understand more than the elders, for I search Your commandments" (Ps 118:100, Septuagint). Wisdom is also acquired through discipleship. We acquire wisdom when we are discipled by wise, experienced elders.

However, I want to discuss wisdom in understanding the nature of man, in general. As a wife, you should understand the general nature of man and the nature and character of your husband, in particular. With this understanding, you will be able to deal with him wisely. Of course, understanding the nature of your husband in particular is your responsibility, but I will give you some points about male psychology, in general.

Male Psychology

The first thing you need to understand about a man is that he fulfills himself through his ability to reach his goals. This is what we call *achievement*. The more he achieves, the more self-confident he feels and the happier he is. A wife who understands this should always encourage and praise her husband for his achievements. If she belittles his achievements, it is as if she is piercing his ego. For example, if he tells her about how hard he worked today and how much he achieved, she may respond by saying something like, "Well, all men work hard; you are not the only one." A wise wife would always acknowledge her husband's achievements and praise and encourage him. She would do this without hypocrisy and mere flattery, because he would not buy it. She needs to be realistic but aware of the achievements in her husband's life.

Secondly, a man is very rational and concentrates on clear and tangible issues that he can measure more than on emotional or humanitarian stories. A woman is not like this; she is emotional. If a wife tells her husband, "I feel that you do not love me," he may not understand this. In his mind, he works hard, earns an income, and takes care of his children and of her, so he believes he is offering love. However, in her mind, he does not love her because he did not buy her a gift for her birthday, or get her roses on Valentine's Day, etc. Thus, when you talk to him in a clear way and mention something tangible as a reason for feeling like he does not love you, i.e., because he did not bring you flowers or buy you a gift, he will be able to understand; it is something he can measure. This will be better for him than unclear, abstract concepts that are not concrete.

The third point is that men tend to be realistic and practical, but women lean toward romanticism and dreams. Whenever they discuss their family budget, whether or not to buy a house, whether to put their children in private or public school, or have any type of discussion like this, the man would be very realistic, adding things up with a paper and pen. If the wife does not understand this point, she may blame him for things he cannot do. Her perception may be unrealistic. I am not just talking about money, but also about taking vacations or going out. For example, if he has a business and cannot take days off, she would say, "You do not love me as you did. We never go out together anymore." He would respond, "This is the way things are right now. I cannot leave my business." Therefore, when you discuss things with your husband, you need to understand that he is realistic. You should understand how he sees things and analyzes life. On the other hand, if I were talking to men, I would tell them something else; I would tell them that they need to get away from strict realism, and meet their wives halfway.

The fourth point is that men do not talk about their feelings. If he has a problem at work, he does not like to talk about it in detail. Most men do not like to burden others with their problems. He carries them around within him, and that is it. A wife may interpret this as him keeping her out of his life. He is not excluding her from his life; it is his nature. Also, he knows what he is going to do to fix it. Even if he shares that he is upset and has a problem at work, and briefly mentions the problem, if she does not understand that this is his nature, she may say, "I do not know why you put barriers between us. Why do you not want to share your life with me? Why do you not tell me about things? I tell you about everything that happens with me at work." There is a difference between the psychology of a man and the psychology of a woman.

Related to this is the fact that when men discuss issues, they do so with concentration and brevity. He does not have the ability to tell details; he speaks briefly and to the point. A wife may feel that he is lying to her, or that he does not love her or want to share with her. Sometimes, when we listen to a problem between a married couple, the wife relays details while the husband speaks in generalities. If asked about the details, he may respond, "I cannot remember exactly." He truly does not remember because his mind is not detail oriented. In this case, a wife may accuse him of dodging the question and point out that he actually has a very good memory. However, this does not mean that he lost his memory. He cannot remember because he does not pay attention to the details. Most men do not focus on the details.

The sixth point in understanding male psychology is that a man has a great need for freedom and independence. He likes to be independent. That is why, from time to time, he steps away for a little while to fulfill this need by perhaps going out with his friends or going fishing. The wife sometimes thinks that this means he does not love her. In fact, I think it is healthy for the husband and the wife, every now and then, to have their own activities. This increases their longing and love for each other. However, a man's need for this is greater than a woman's need for it. Of course, if he does this too often—for example, if he is out every week with his friends and is not spending time at home or with his wife and children—this is wrong. I am saying that this need is there every now and then, and the wife should not interpret this in a wrong way.

The seventh point is if a conflict occurs between the husband and wife and they make up, the man usually goes back to the point before the fight. However, a woman may go back to square one. She wants to start all over and build life between them from scratch. This can cause a clash between them. She may say things like, "Do you think that just because you apologized, this means that everything can go back to normal? Do you think that saying sorry erases everything you did, and all the yelling and fighting?" He apologized and wants life to move on; she takes time for healing. This is a psychological difference. I am not saying one is right and the other is wrong, but we are trying to understand male psychology.

The more wisdom a wife has, and the more she understands the psychology of her husband, the more she can gain him to God. The wisdom of the woman builds her house.

How to Win Over Your Husband

In order to win over your husband, there are certain things you must avoid, no matter the cost.

Contention

The first thing you need to avoid is contention. Sometimes, a person needs to let things go. People should not get upset and hold grudges about everything; otherwise, life will be difficult to bear. If either spouse gets upset quite often, sometimes without any realistic explanation, this puts a lot of stress on the marital relationship. This is why the Holy Bible warned women about contention. I will share with you some verses. "Better to dwell in a corner of a housetop, than in a house shared with a contentious woman" (Prov 21:9). If someone lives in a small room on a housetop, this is better than living in a big house with contention. Of course, these verses can also be applied to husbands. "Better to dwell in the wilderness, than with a contentious and angry woman" (Prov 21:19). "A continual dripping on a very rainy day and a contentious woman are alike" (Prov 27:15). Also, the Holy Bible warned us about contention when it said, "Do not let the sun go down on your wrath, nor give place to the devil" (Eph 4:26–27). When we become contentious, we invite the devil to enter the house. Contention means that we give the devil permission to come and dwell with us.

Contention has different forms, such as giving snappy answers or avoiding the other person. For example, he goes to work at a certain time, so she sleeps until he leaves. Contention could also be clear, such as refusing to speak to each other. Other forms include being upset, or leaving home and going to her parents' house; when she is upset, she goes to her family.

The Holy Bible teaches us how to reconcile, and gives precedence to reconciliation over anything else, even worship: "Therefore if you bring your gift to the altar, and there remember that your brother has something against you, leave your gift there before the altar, and go your way. First be reconciled to your brother, and then come and offer your gift" (Mt 5:24–25). Thus, it is better to agree together to give priority to reconciliation and resolving arguments. Disagreements should not remain until the next day. If they remain, everyone will be affected; the wife will be upset, the husband will be upset, and if the children feel it, they will be upset. There will be no peace in the house.

Revenge and Punishment

The second thing to avoid is punishment and revenge. A man punishes

184

someone either by using aggression (yelling and anger), or, if he has control over the finances, by saying that he will take away the credit card and checkbook. Women have other ways; they tend to be more passive-aggressive. Sometimes, the spirit of anger creates a desire for revenge. We can say that revenge is strong anger mixed with a feeling of oppression and helplessness and a desire to avenge oneself. I will give you some examples of what a wife does to take revenge. She may expose his faults in front of his family, her family, the priest, and his friends at church. I was solving a problem last week between a newly married couple of six months. They had a disagreement, and she told Abouna, their friends, her family, his family, and me. When he sat down with us, he said, "What was the reason for all of this? Could Abouna not have solved this problem by himself?" He was upset that the problem had reached all those people in less than 48 hours. Bringing in a third party is called triangulation. It is a mechanism used to offset the balance and alleviate the stress of one side by having another for support.

Other ways to take revenge include refusing to help with the household budget and excessively spending money. Or, she may expose him on Facebook. Unfortunately, it is common to punish or take revenge by refraining from the marital relationship, and this causes major problems. Also, she may incite the children against him and distort their image of him. She can get the children's sympathy against their father. Some wives may justify getting involved in an emotional relationship with another man. Also, if her responsibilities at home involve cooking, cleaning, and laundry, she may exclude his things from those chores. All of these are various forms of punishment and revenge.

We read in the Book of Proverbs that the righteous woman "does him good and not evil all the days of her life" (Prov 31:12). This is a very nice verse. I wish that all wives would examine themselves against this verse. Also, St. Paul says, "Repay no one evil for evil ... Beloved, do not avenge yourselves, but rather give place to wrath; for it is written, 'Vengeance is Mine, I will repay,' says the Lord" (Rom 12:17, 19). Judgment, vengeance, and punishment are the Lord's, not ours. The most we can do is discipline, meaning that a parent can discipline his children and a teacher his students. However, vengeance is God's responsibility, not our responsibility.

Doubt

A third thing we need to avoid is doubt. We may not only doubt his moral behavior, but also many other things: "He is hiding his income from me," or, "He is keeping money in Egypt and I do not know about it." The root of suspicion is absolute trust in one's own personal intelligence. Someone would say, "I know very well what is going on. Even if I do not have proof, I am certain he is doing that." This is absolute trust in her personal intelligence. Doubt provides a fertile opportunity for the devil to divide the spouses and build a wall between them. Usually, if doubt enters the relationship, we get caught in a vicious cycle that does not end in any other way other than the destruction of the home. If she is suspicious about everything, especially his behavior, this can result in the demise of the family.

The treatment for doubt is to differentiate between feelings and reality. A wife should not rely on her feelings to accuse her husband without proof. Even if your feelings make you certain, and if I assume your feelings are correct, there will eventually be evidence. No one does something wrong without leaving behind evidence. They always say that there is no crime without evidence. Therefore, instead of just acting on your feelings, wait. If your feelings are correct, you will have the evidence. Then, we can talk. If there is no evidence, it is better not to talk. On many occasions, feelings are misleading, and the devil can use these opportunities.

You may ask, "What should I do about the thoughts that keep fighting me? I cannot get rid of them." You need to stop interacting with these thoughts. If you were struggling with sinful thoughts, you would deal with them by rejecting them and staying busy with something else, so that the thoughts would not cling to you. If thoughts are pulling someone in one direction, he must find something else, stronger than the thoughts, to pull him in the opposite direction. This is one of the best treatments for thoughts. When someone tells me that thoughts are bothering him, I tell him to go out and talk to someone about anything (not for the sake of complaining about the situation). This way, you will not pay attention to the thoughts. Do not remain alone, because if you do, the thought will control you. However, if you distract the thought, it will not overcome you.

These thoughts are from the enemy. St. James says, "Resist the devil and he will flee from you" (Jas 4:7). When you keep forcing out a thought, it will not return to you. The Church Fathers compare the devil to a dog that keeps going back to the butcher. If the butcher shoos the dog away every time, he will not return. However, if he feeds him, the dog will stay and not leave. It is the same with the devil; if you accept the thought, he will stay, but if I kick him out every time by the power of the cross, and rebuke him with the power of the Holy Spirit in me, the devil will leave. "Resist the devil and he will flee from you."

Jealousy

The fourth thing to avoid is jealousy. St. Paul the Apostle listed jealousy as one of the works of the flesh: "Now the works of the flesh are evident, which are: adultery, fornication, uncleanness, lewdness, idolatry, sorcery, hatred, contentions, jealousies, outbursts of wrath, selfish ambitions, dissensions, heresies, envy, murders, drunkenness, revelries, and the like; of which I tell you beforehand, just as I also told you in time past, that those who practice such things will not inherit the kingdom of God" (Gal 5:19–21). Therefore, jealousy may forbid me from inheriting the kingdom of God. "For wrath kills a foolish man, and envy slays a simple one" (Job 5:2). A person who lacks wisdom and gives himself over to jealousy could be killed by this jealousy. Also, when St. James differentiated between heavenly wisdom and sensual earthly wisdom, he said, "For where envy and self-seeking exist, confusion and every evil thing are there" (Jas 3:16). Jealousy can be destructive to the relationship between the husband and wife.

The roots of jealousy are lack of self-confidence and feelings of insecurity. It is the opposite of the root of doubt, which is absolute trust in one's personal intelligence. If there were two servants serving together and one was insecure, he would become jealous of the other. Also, if there is insecurity and lack of self-confidence at home, this could turn into jealousy.

Jealousy has different forms. It could be jealousy *of* someone or *for* someone. For example, a wife could be jealous *of* her mother-in-law; in this case, there would be a competition between her and her mother-in-law. This competition could be over trivial issues, such as whose food is better, who dresses better, etc. This could lead to arguments. It could also be jealousy *for* her husband. She may say, "You always call your mother on the phone and speak to her freely. Why don't you call me when we have been apart for a while?" Or, "You are always at church and in the service. If Abouna calls you, of course you answer him immediately, but if I ask for something, I have to wait for weeks until you do it." In these examples, you can sense the lack of self-confidence. She feels unloved and unimportant. Jealousy can harm the home.

Contempt and Disrespect

The fifth thing to avoid is disrespect (or contempt), which can be explicit or implicit. Inside herself, she may look down on him. Even if she does not say the words, her behavior, her way of talking, and her method of dealing with him and with her children, sends a message that her husband does not measure up to her expectations. Some wives have expressed these sentiments. I have heard it from them: "He embarrasses me everywhere." "I am ashamed of him." "I do not like him to be around me." This reminds me of Michal, the daughter of Saul: "Now as the ark of the Lord came into the City of David, Michal, Saul's daughter, looked through a window and saw King David leaping and whirling before the Lord; and she despised him in her heart" (2 Sam 6:16). "Then David returned to bless his household. And Michal the daughter of Saul came out to meet David, and said, 'How glorious was the king of Israel today, uncovering himself today in the eyes of the maids of his servants, as one of the base fellows shamelessly uncovers himself!'" (2 Sam 6:20).

When a young man proposes to a young woman and there is a difference between them, whether in education, age (if she is several years older than him), income, or in social status, I often worry that after some time, when the emotions settle down and they encounter real life, she would look down on him and despise him, especially if she has a higher position, more intelligence, or a higher salary. This could lead to disrespect, even internally.

What would make a woman despise her husband? Comparing him to other men, even in her mind, could cause her to disrespect him. For example, she may compare him to her boss at work and note how her boss is an achiever and a leader. If her husband does not have these traits, she may start to despise him in her heart. Also, if he cannot meet her high financial goals, she may despise him. Or, perhaps she cannot accept that he has certain weaknesses. She may have pride and feel that she is better than him socially, financially, or spiritually. If she is an active servant in church and is loved, and her husband does not go to church, she may despise him because she perceives him in a less spiritual level as she is. In this case, she would need to reevaluate her own spiritual life. Does her spiritual life teach her to despise her husband? Does despising her husband fit with this high level of spirituality or is it a matter of feeling superior to him?

She may also despise him regarding his sensual or physical desires. I do not want to talk much about this topic, but the physical relationship is important for men. Romantic words and emotions are more important for the wife than physical intimacy. When he has a physical desire, she may make comments that imply that she despises him. "Can you not control yourself?" Such comments go back to the point I mentioned that she does not understand male psychology. Such comments are degrading to a man.

Respect is important to men. That is why St. Paul says, "Let each one of you in particular so love his own wife as himself, and let the wife see that she respects her husband" (Eph 5:33). This is because love is very important for women, and respect is very important for men. Being abased can hurt a husband immensely. What are the signs of a wife's disrespect? If he is talking, especially in front of other people, she may interrupt him, correct him, or make fun of him. If she speaks another language well but he does not, she may ridicule him. Or, if she speaks a language he does not understand, she may speak it with her friends in front of him. She may disobey him in front of the children. Also, talking to him in a loud voice, giving him orders, rebuking or blaming him in front of others, criticizing him, downgrading his achievements, and using guilt messages to make him feel that he is not doing enough are all signs of disrespect and contempt.

A Crafty Tongue

The sixth thing to avoid is a crafty tongue. "A soft answer turns away wrath, but a harsh word stirs up anger" (Prov 15:1). "A word fitly spoken is like apples of gold in settings of silver" (Prov 25:11). I remember sitting with a couple over sixty years of age and were grandparents. They were getting a divorce. I was astonished that they were getting a divorce after such a long time. The husband said, "I cannot tolerate this any longer. Every morning when I am leaving for work, she curses me." She does not bless him, but curses him and he hears her. When I confronted her, she did not deny it, but justified it by saying that it was because of the kind of person he was. A crafty tongue is very tiresome. I hope we train ourselves to utter words of gratitude, words of blessing and not cursing, words expressing love, encouragement, and praise. All of this has a pleasant effect. It creates a loving and respectful environment in the home. Even if the person in front of you is angry, he will calm down with a kind word.

Overburdening Each Other with Financial Requests

The last thing to avoid is overburdening him with financial needs. The Holy Bible praises the economical wife: "She seeks wool and flax, and willingly works with her hands. She is like the merchant ships, she brings her food from afar. She also rises while it is yet night, and provides food for her household, and a portion for her maidservants. She considers a field and buys it; from her profits she plants a vineyard (Prov 31:13–16). These beautiful verses show how a woman can be economical. However, some women envy others and want to buy a house or a car just because someone else did. Or, someone got a diamond for her birthday, so she wants the same. All of this is under the umbrella of the pride of life and an unnecessary financial burden to the household. This is wrong. Some men say that they feel that their wives want them to be a money machine, just providing them with money so they can be satisfied with them as husbands. Otherwise, there will be fighting, yelling, and misery at home.

If we avoid these seven points, contention, punishment and revenge, doubt, jealousy, disrespect, a crafty tongue, and overburdening each other with financial requests, the couple will create an environment of peace and love.

In conclusion, I remind you that St. Peter says that God has given the woman a very great ability to win over her husband by her behavior. "If some do not obey the word," meaning that even if some husbands do not obey the word of God, "they, without a word, may be won by the conduct of their wives, when they observe" (since you win him over without a word) "your chaste conduct accompanied by fear" (1 Pet 3:1–2).

14 Relationships with Family Members (Homily to Youth)

The Difficulty of Honoring our Parents

Principles of Honor

Honor is a Parent's God-Given Right

Honoring Parents is a Social Matter

How to Honor our Parents

Listen

Respect their Role

Value their Advice

Meet their Needs

Affirm their Efforts

Forgive their Failings

Imitate them in the Way of God

Communicate

Do Not Speak Badly to or About Them

Remind them that you Care

Usually, we speak with parents about how to deal with adolescents, and we give them instructions about how to deal wisely with them. On the other hand, it is very rare to speak with college students or adolescents about how to deal with their parents. We often think that the commandment to honor your father and your mother is intended for little children, not for adolescents and adults. The fact is, this commandment is not related to a specific age, but God gave this commandment to all people of all ages.

The Difficulty of Honoring our Parents

As we get older, obeying our parents becomes one of the most difficult things to do, especially as teenagers. When we become adolescents and want to differentiate ourselves from our parents and perceive ourselves as adults, the first thing we do is rebel against authority. The first authority we rebel against is our parents. For the first twelve years of our lives, we listen to them, obey them, and follow their instructions. Now, it is time to feel like an adult. We do not want them to tell us what to do because we are adults and independent. We feel that it is time to do things on our own and we want to prove that we are responsible adults. We believe that we do not need our parents anymore, but the fact is, there is still a level on which we need them. In fact, it is not only about needing them, but it is also a commandment, which means that we should honor our parents regardless of whether we need them or not. God told us to honor our parents.

Why is it challenging for us to respect or obey our parents at this age? First, most of us believe that we do not need them anymore. Many of us believe that we are wiser than our parents, especially regarding technology and because our experience here in America may be greater than theirs. That is why we justify disrespecting and dishonoring them.

Secondly, unfortunately, most of us grow up with a critical eye toward our parents, which is why we do not honor them. Maybe their English is not as good as ours. Maybe it is because they are from Egypt, and we understand the culture here better than they do. Maybe we believe that our parents are not righteous and godly, or that they are too busy for us and do not give us their time and attention. We have all of these excuses: "My parents are too harsh on me. They are over-protective. They do not understand what I am going through." Obeying our parents is not easy; it is hard. It is a challenge, especially at this age.

The Holy Bible tells us that when we obey our parents, this grants us wisdom. In the Book of Proverbs, we read, "The fear of the Lord is the beginning of knowledge, but fools despise wisdom and instruction. My son, hear the instruction of your father, and do not forsake the law of your mother; for they will be a graceful ornament on your head, and chains about your neck" (Prov 1:7–9). In these three verses, the Holy Bible tells us that when we listen to our parents, we will acquire wisdom, and they can lead us in the path of God. Their advice is *very* valuable. You should know that our parents offer advice and discipline out of love. Nobody else will have the same love for me that my parents do. That is why our reaction to this love should be to listen to them and to learn from everything they tell us.

Also, obeying and honoring our parents will make us more faithful and bring us closer to God. Why did God use the term "Father" to describe Himself? When we address Him, we say, "Our Father who art in heaven." Also, why did God liken Himself to a mother? He said, "Can a woman forget her nursing child, and not have compassion on the son of her womb? Surely they may forget, yet I will not forget you" (Is 49:15). It is because God wants us to obey Him as we obey our parents. How can we obey our heavenly Father if we cannot obey our earthly parents? If we say that we obey our heavenly Father, but we do not obey our earthly parents whom we see, we are lying and deceive ourselves. When we learn how to obey our parents, our eyes and our ears will be opened to God's plan for us. Thus, I can say that obedience is the first step in living a Christian life, and it helps me to be strong in my faith. As I learn how to obey my parents, I will know how to obey God. That is why obeying and honoring my parents will teach me how to obey God and get closer to Him.

Principles of Honor

Honor is a Parent's God-Given Right

Receiving honor is a right given to parents by God. Parents are entitled to it, which is why it is considered a sin to disrespect them.

> And even as they did not like to retain God in their knowledge, God gave them over to a debased mind, to do those things which are not fitting; being filled with all unrighteousness, sexual immorality, wickedness, covetousness, maliciousness; full of envy, murder, strife, deceit, evil-mindedness; they are whisperers, backbiters, haters of God, violent, proud, boasters, inventors of evil things, disobedient to parents, undiscerning, untrustworthy, unloving, unforgiving, unmerciful; who, knowing the righteous judgment of God, that those who practice such things are deserving of death, not only do the same but also approve of those who practice them (Rom 1:28–32).

God, through St. Paul, listed disobedience to parents among sins such as sexual immorality, wickedness, hatred of God, murder, and strife, and St. Paul said that the wrath of God will come upon those who practice these sins. Therefore, disobedience to parents is a sin that is no less than murder or adultery, since these sins are all grouped into one category. We also read:

> But know this, that in the last days perilous times will come: For men will be lovers of themselves, lovers of money, boasters, proud, blasphemers, disobedient to parents, unthankful, unholy, unloving, unforgiving, slanderers, without self-control, brutal, despisers of good, traitors, headstrong, haughty, lovers of pleasure rather than lovers of God, having a form of godliness but denying its power. And from such people turn away! (2 Tim 3:1–5).

Again, St. Paul listed disobedience to parents among sins such as loving money, pride, blasphemy, etc. He also described it as a sign of the last days. In other words, one of the signs of the last days is that children will be rebellious and disobey their parents.

These verses tell us that disobedience to parents is a major sin. Disobedience to parents also generates more sins. How so? Parents' advice is very valuable, and it will help you do the right thing. Therefore, when you disobey them, you will do things that are wrong. I am sure that all of you know that the Ten Commandments are ordered according to importance. The first four commandments regulate our relationship with God and the last six regulate our relationship with one another. After God spoke about how to deal with Him in the first four commandments, the first commandment in dealing with one another is: "Honor your father and your mother" (Ex 20:12). God put this commandment before "You shall not murder," "You shall not commit adultery," "You shall not steal," "You shall not bear false witness," and "You shall not covet." He put it before all of the other commandments, as if God is telling us, "If you fail to honor your parents, you will most probably fail to keep the other commandments." That is why He put it as the first commandment of the second tablet, which regulates our relationships with others. Therefore, honoring your parents is the first step in living a Christian life.

Honoring parents is also the first commandment with a promise: "'Honor your father and mother,' which is the first commandment with promise: 'that it may be well with you and you may live long on the earth'" (Eph 6:2–3). The promise has two dimensions: "That it may be well with you" and that "you may live long on the earth." God gave us a promise if we keep this commandment, and there is a punishment if we do not keep it. If we do not honor our parents, according to the Holy Bible, God instructed that this son or daughter would be killed: "He who strikes his father or his mother shall surely be put to death ... And he who curses his father or his mother shall surely be put to death" (Ex 21:15, 17). I wonder if this verse were applied literally, how many of us would not be alive today? Moreover, if God made the punishment for this sin death, this means that honoring our parents is a very serious matter.

God wants us to honor parents because they are His representatives. When we honor them, we are honoring God. If we rebel against them, we are rebelling against God. They are His stewards, and stewards represent their master. God, as a Master, entrusted stewards with gifts; He entrusted our parents with the gift of children. We are God's gift to our parents.

God also broadened the meaning of parents. The word "parents" does not only refer to our biological parents, but also includes all adults and elders. We read in Leviticus 19:32, "You shall rise before the gray headed and honor the presence of an old man, and fear your God: I am the Lord." You shall stand before them out of respect. For example, it would not be proper for you to remain seated while there is an elderly person standing. You should rise before him and give him your place. The Holy Bible teaches you how to respect the elderly. When an old man is speaking, you cannot interrupt him. You should listen to him and respect his presence.

Honoring Parents is a Social Matter

In Deuteronomy chapter 21, it is very clear that in biblical times, people regarded disrespectful and rebellious children as a problem for the entire society, one that the whole society had to address—as the common saying says, "As the home goes, so goes the nation." If children in the family are rebellious, the whole society will become rebellious; if children are disrespectful in the family, the whole nation will be disrespectful.

> If a man has a stubborn and rebellious son who will not obey the voice of his father or the voice of his mother, and who, when they have chastened him, will not heed them, then his father and his mother shall take hold of him and bring him out to the elders of his city, to the gate of his city. And they shall say to the elders of his city, "This son of ours is stubborn and rebellious; he will not obey our voice; he is a glutton and a drunkard." Then all the men of his city shall stone him to death with stones; so you shall put away the evil from among you, and all Israel shall hear and fear (Deut 21:18–21).

In these verses, if a father and mother bore witness against their child, that he is rebellious and disrespectful, they would bring him to the gate of the city. They would bring the elders, and then all the people would stone this person to death. The reason that God gave for this is to "put away the evil from among you." Having a rebellious spirit is evil. God wants to say that if you keep a rebellious or disrespectful son, this is an evil and it may ruin the entire nation. He would set a bad example and other children would learn to be rebellious. Moreover, if children do not know how to obey their parents, they would not know how to respect any authority; thus, the whole community would become corrupted, filled with rebellious children and people who rebel against the law and every authority. If the whole community were full of rebellious children, it would be a corrupted community. That is why you need to put away the evil from among you.

If we know how to respect authority in our homes, we will know how to respect authority in the whole community. However, if we do not know how to respect authority in our own houses, we will never know how to respect other authority.

I am sure that while you are reading this now, some of you are thinking that this is not practical. "My parents do not understand me." "My parents deal very harshly with me." "My parents try to control me." "They are overprotective." "How are you asking me to obey them?" I will give you some tips to help you understand your parents and how to honor them practically.

How to Honor our Parents

Listen

Listen. One of the easiest ways to learn from your parents and to be able to honor them is to listen to what they have to say. How can you obey them when you do not actually hear what they are telling you? When you start listening to them and take the time to absorb what they are telling you, the things you will hear from them will amaze you.

When Samson was your age, or a little bit older, he decided to marry a girl outside of his faith. His parents gave him advice, but he did not listen to it. Samson made three mistakes in his marriage. First, he married someone outside his faith. Second, he made his decision based on physical attraction. Third, he did not listen to his parents' advice or even discuss the matter with them. He simply disregarded what they told him.

His parents asked him why he was marrying someone from the uncircumcised peoples (see Judg 14:3). In the Old Testament, circumcision was a symbol of being God's people. It was a symbol of baptism. When his parents asked him why he was marrying someone from the uncircumcised people, they meant people who were foreigners to God, who worshipped idols and not the true God.

Nowadays, we can replace the word *uncircumcised* with *unbaptized*, since circumcision is a symbol of baptism. If you bring someone who is an atheist or from a different religion or denomination to your parents, they would ask how you could marry someone from another faith. However, we do not listen to them or even discuss it with them. If you know Samson's story, his wife ended up deceiving him, and he got angry and left her. Then, (without Samson knowing), her father gave her as a wife to Samson's friend, who had been his best man in his wedding. When Samson came to ask for his wife back, her father told him that they had already given her to another man and that if he wanted, he could marry her sister. Samson got really upset and burned the fields of the Philistines. This marriage failed. One reason for this failure is because Samson did not listen to his parents. He thought he was wiser than them. He was a Nazirite to the Lord; therefore, he thought he was wiser and did not need to listen to them.

Listen to your parents. When they talk to you, do not turn away or leave them. Do not turn a deaf ear. Listen to them.

Respect their Role

We need to respect our parents' role. Honoring a person means to respect him as someone who carries a great deal of weight in your life. Respect your parents as people who carry a great deal of weight in your life. Show them respect. There is nothing more frustrating to a parent than when he or she is talking to his or her child and he just walks away or rolls his eyes. Maybe you do not agree with their advice. Maybe they do not understand you. Maybe they are ungodly. However, these are not an excuses for you to disrespect them. Even if you disagree or need clarification, you can discuss this in a respectful way. When you insist on your opinion, raise your voice over them, argue, or scream, it is unlikely that your parents will listen to your objection. Disrespect will immediately create a wall between you and your parents. Moreover, displeases God when you do not respect your parents, this.

In the Book of Genesis, after God saved Noah and his family from the flood, there is a story that I am sure all of you know. "Noah began to be a farmer, and he planted a vineyard. Then, he drank its wine, got drunk, and became uncovered in his tent" (Gen 9:20–21). Noah brought this upon himself; because he was intoxicated, his body was exposed. Therefore, I can say that Noah did something wrong here. "And Ham, the father of Canaan, saw the nakedness of his father" (Gen 9:22). Ham should have covered his father, but, in fact, Ham disrespected his father, and he went and told his two brothers who were outside. How did his brothers react? "But Shem and Japheth took a garment, laid it on both their shoulders, and went backward and covered the nakedness of their father" (Gen 9:23). Can you picture what they did? They held a sheet, walked backwards, and covered their father. They did this in order to not see his nakedness, as a matter of respect. "Their faces were turned away, and they did not see their father's nakedness" (Gen 9:23). Here, there are two sons who were respectful to their father, even when he did something wrong— he became drunk—but one son was disrespectful to his father.

"So Noah awoke from his wine, and knew what his younger son had done to him. Then he said: 'Cursed be Canaan; a servant of servants he shall be to his brethren.' And he said: 'Blessed be the Lord, the God of Shem, and may Canaan be his servant. May God enlarge Japheth, and may he dwell in the tents of Shem; and may Canaan be his servant'" (Gen 9:24–27). If you study the history, you will find that the children of Shem and Japheth were in fact blessed by God, but the children of Canaan were not because of what they did to their father. This means that God fulfilled what Noah said, because God wants us to honor our parents and show them respect.

Parents are appointed by God. They are His representatives and He entrusted them to be our teachers and guides. "For He established a testimony in Jacob, and appointed a law in Israel, which He commanded our fathers, that they should make them known to their children; that the generation to come might know them, the children who would be born, that they may arise and declare them to their children, that they may set their hope in God, and not forget the works of God, but keep His commandments" (Ps 78:5–7). God made it very clear that it is the parents' responsibility to teach their children His commandments and to guide them according to His law. This is an awesome responsibility. That is why we need to respect them and honor them. We need to speak to them with courtesy and respect. "He who mistreats his father and chases away his mother is a son who causes shame and brings reproach" (Prov 19:26).

There is a common saying in Arabic, "He who teaches me one letter, I will become his servant." Our parents do not only teach us one letter, but they teach us *life*—how to be good people, good Christians, and good citizens. If I will become a servant to the person who teaches me one letter, how much more honor should I have for my parents?

Furthermore, if our parents ask us to do anything, we should listen to them. In the miracle of transforming water into wine, St. Mary noticed that there was a problem and asked the Lord Jesus Christ to help. The Lord told her, "My hour has not yet come" (Jn 2:4), which means that He should not start now. However, despite the fact that His hour had not yet come, He obeyed her and did what she asked Him to do, meaning that the Lord was not stubborn. In fact, she did not even tell him to solve the problem, but just stating the problem conveyed her concern, but He did not tell her, "My hour has not yet come, so just leave Me alone. I know better. I am God, your Creator." This is a great lesson for us about how to respect our parents' role. We should obey when they ask us to do something, and we should respect their authority.

Value their Advice

Value their advice because it is God's advice. Sometimes, we despise our parents' advice and we believe that we know better. "A wise son heeds his father's instruction, but a scoffer does not listen to rebuke" (Prov 13:1). This verse tells us that it is foolishness to not heed to your father's instructions. "Children, obey your parents in *all things*, for this is well pleasing to the Lord" (Col 3:20, emphasis added). When you obey your parents, God will be pleased with you. However, disobeying them will displease the Lord. "Children, obey your parents in the Lord, for this is right" (Eph 6:1). Obedience to our parents should be part of our obedience to the Lord, and should not contradict our obedience to Him. If my parents ask me to do something against the commandment of God, I should excuse myself very politely and nicely, not in a judgmental way.

We need to obey them in the Lord because God has placed them in authority over us. Valuing their advice is the right thing to do, pleases God, and is a symbol of wisdom.

Meet their Needs

You need to take care of them when it is within your ability, not only when they are old and in need of you, but by doing simple things right now according to your ability. For example, if you are sitting together at the table, is it respectful to ask your father or mother to bring you a cup of water or a spoon? It is not right to give them orders and ask them to get you things. In fact, the opposite should be done: *You* should serve *them*. "He who mistreats his father and chases away his mother is a son who causes shame and brings reproach" (Prov 19:26). The phrase "mistreats his father" may refer to not giving your parents' *their* rights.

Archangel Gabriel told Zacharias, in reference to the birth of St. John the Baptist, "You will have joy and gladness, and many will rejoice at his birth" (Lk 1:14). I want you to ask yourselves, "Am I a source of joy and happiness to my parents? Or, am I a source of shame and bitterness to them?" When Zacharias and Elizabeth remembered John the Baptist, they were joyful and happy because of their son; they were proud of him. However, some children are a source of bitterness to their parents and their parents feel ashamed and unhappy because of them. If I am a source of bitterness, how can I change this to become a source of joy for my parents?

Also, in 1 Timothy 5:4, St. Paul puts religion into practice by caring for one's own family: "If any widow has children or grandchildren, let them first learn to show piety at home and to repay their parents; for this is good and acceptable before God." During the time of St. Paul, a widow had no support because men were the main breadwinners. If a widow had children or grandchildren, it was their responsibility to take care of her. This is acceptable to God; this pleases God. If they do not do this, they are not spiritual or religious. You are neither spiritual nor religious if your parents are in need and you are able to help them but do not. For example, if you work and make money during the summer, and your parents need some money, but you do not want to give it to them, you are not meeting their needs, and this is not right. You cannot call yourself religious in this way.

The Lord Jesus Christ set an example of how to meet the needs of one's parents. Consider what He did with His mother. "When Jesus therefore saw His mother, and the disciple whom He loved standing by, He said to His mother, 'Woman, behold your son!' Then He said to the disciple, 'Behold your mother!' And from that hour that disciple took her to his own home" (Jn 19:26–27). God took care of His mother even in the time of His suffering, when He was on the cross. This was a *very* painful moment for Him. He had attended six trials on the previous night and had not slept the entire night. He was scourged and beaten and went through many sufferings. After all of this, they nailed Him to the cross and He was about to die. If the Lord Jesus Christ had not remembered His mother at that moment, no one would blame Him because there was a very good reason— He was going through severe pain and agony. Agony, because the sins of the whole world were placed on Him, and pain because of the suffering of crucifixion. However, in the midst of all the physical and psychological pain, He did not forget His mother. This is a great lesson to us about how to meet the needs of our parents, even in our difficult times. We should not ask our parents to leave us alone when we have finals, for example. The Lord did not tell His mother, "I am dying now—just leave Me alone."

Affirm their Efforts

Appreciate them. Show them that you appreciate what they do for you. If you always complain and give them a hard time, and do not show appreciation, this is not affirming their efforts. How many times have you told your parents, "Thank you?" "Listen to your father who begot you, and do not despise your mother when she is old" (Prov 23:22). Show them that you appreciate everything they have done and that you really love them. Many children make their parents feel guilty about what they have done to them. Sometimes, we consider our parents old-fashioned; we think that they do not understand, and we laugh at them because they do not speak English as well as we do and do not understand the culture. We may tell them that they are Egyptian, backwards, old-fashioned, and that we cannot wait until we move out of the house, etc. We believe that we are from an advanced culture, so how could people who come from a backwards country advise us and tell us what to do? We often despise their advice and believe that we know better than them. Is this how to affirm their efforts? If you are bragging because you are American and grew up in America, this is because *your parents* brought you here. You would never have seen America if your parents had not come here. Also remember, that their decision to immigrate to a foreign country was most likely to provide better opportunities for you and your future, despite the hardships they would have to endure. After they have done all of this, do not hold it against them and laugh at them, despise them, mock them, and give them a hard time. This is not right. You need to affirm their efforts.

When your parents are old, and you have grown up, show them your appreciation. When King Solomon's mother came to meet with him, Solomon, who was a king and sitting on the royal throne, did the following: "Bathsheba therefore went to King Solomon, to speak to him for Adonijah. And the king rose up to meet her and bowed down to her, and sat down on his throne and had a throne set for the king's mother; so she sat at his right hand" (1 Kg 2:19). He honored his mother.

Forgive their Failings

Your parents are human beings. They are imperfect, and they will make mistakes. However, I want to promise you that no one in the whole world loves you as much as your parents do, even if they are overprotective sometimes and do not give you the freedom that you want, or if they do not trust you sometimes and give you a hard time.

Have patience with them. Most parents of teenagers are now in their forties or early fifties, and they experience a lot of pressure at this age. For example, many companies squeeze workers out at this age and put a lot of pressure on them. This is because people in their sixties are starting to think about retirement, and people younger than this, in their thirties, are beginners and gaining experience. Therefore, there is a very high level of stress at work. Moreover, most of parents at this age also have parents who are getting older and probably retired and may need a lot of attention.

Think about your parents: They have pressure from work. They have pressure from your grandparents because they need a lot of attention from them, and they have pressure from you. You are growing and becoming teenagers, and have demands. In addition to this, there is also pressure from society. At this age, they might be very active in church, whether in Sunday school, on the board of deacons, or with other activities. This is beside the fact that hormonal and physical changes occur in the forties and fifties, and these parents are dealing with their own physiological changes. Thus, the level of stress at this age is very difficult for them.

Because teenagers and young adults probably do not understand their parents' challenges, they tend to be impatient with them and immediately snap at them for everything. It is easy to hold grudges when they are wrong. We forget that our parents are human beings just like us. The Holy Bible tells us that to be forgiven, we have to forgive. If you do not forgive, you will not be forgiven. You need to be willing to forgive and forget. Without forgiveness, you remain stuck in anger. I hear many youth say, "I cannot forgive my parents for what they did in my life," or, "I will never forget what my dad did to me." This is not right. God forgives you, and your parents forgive you repeatedly.

Do you know what? In a few years, when you get married and become parents, most of you will fall in the same mistakes that your parents made, because you are human beings just as they are. Obeying and honoring our parents means that we accept that they are not perfect; we accept that they are human beings just like us. Our parents make mistakes, too. When we are patient with them and understand that they will do things incorrectly often, we can learn from their mistakes, as we can learn from our own mistakes. You should be willing to forgive your parents. Do not hold these mistakes against them nor be judgmental or very harsh toward them.

Let me share with you a personal experience. Sometimes, when we are outsiders, we can judge the behavior of others as wrong, but when we are in the same position or responsibility, we act like them. When I was your age, many times I wondered why Abouna was doing certain things the way he did. I would think to myself that perhaps if he had done it differently, it would have been better. When I became a priest, I started doing what I previously criticized in him. Back then, I thought I was wiser than Abouna and I believed that he should have done things differently. When I became a priest, I realized that what he was doing was right. In the same way, I later started asking, "Why are the bishops doing it that way?" According to my judgment, I thought it would have been better if they did certain things differently. Then, when I became a bishop, I started doing exactly what they had done, because it was the right way to do things. As children, we may say this about our parents. "Why do they think like this? Why are they doing things like that? They are overprotective. Why do they want to check on me? Why do they want me to text them when I am late?" When you become a parent, you will do the same things. Be patient and understanding with them. They are not super-humans; they are just human beings like you.

Imitate them in the Way of God

Follow how they go to church, pray, read the Holy Bible, and have a good relationship with God. Any person in the world has positive and negative characteristics. Imitate them in the right way, as St. Paul says, "Obey your parents in the Lord" (Eph 6:1). For example, when you see them wake up early on Sunday to go to church, learn this from them. When you see your mother wake up early in the morning and pray from her Agpeya, learn this from her. When you see your father read his Bible every night before he goes to sleep, learn this.

St. Paul said to Timothy, "But you must continue in the things which you have learned and been assured of, knowing from whom you have learned them, and that from childhood you have known the Holy Scriptures, which are able to make you wise for salvation through faith which is in Christ Jesus" (2 Tim 3:14–15). Many people believe that St. Paul is speaking about himself in these verses, but this is not the case. He does not mean for Timothy to continue in the things that he had learned from him. St. Paul mentions how Timothy has known the Holy Scriptures from *childhood,* and St. Paul did not know Timothy in his childhood; he met Timothy when he was sixteen. Timothy learned his faith from his mother and grandmother, and this is whom St. Paul means when he says, "knowing from whom you have learned them." At that time, St. Timothy was the bishop of Ephesus; thus, St. Paul was telling a bishop to continue in what he [Timothy] had learned from his [Timothy's] parents.

Communicate

We often stop communicating when we start feeling that we are independent. For example, if you going to be late past your curfew, call them and let them know. What is wrong with that? Is it because now you are grown up and should not have a curfew? It is not about setting boundaries; it is about your safety. When your child is late, you will be worried and wondering if something happened to him. Why does it bother you to text or call them, instead of turning your phone off and making it so they are unable to reach you? Does communicating with them make you not an adult? Does it make you immature? A child? Of course not. If they ask you to do something and you will not do it, why do you not communicate that with them and explain to that you will be unable to do whatever that is, in a respectful way? Communication is a key element in having a good relationship with our parents.

When you communicate with them and let them know what is going on in your life, they will accept that you are now becoming an adult and have responsibilities. By communicating with them, you prove to them that you are a responsible person, so they can trust you and have faith in you. Communication is evidence that you are a responsible adult. Not communicating means that you are irresponsible, regardless of your age.

Moreover, there is nothing wrong with asking them for advice. Talk to them about school, your major, and your career. If they do not have experience in that area, you can ask for their prayers. When they listen to you, you will receive compassion, support, and understanding from them.

Adolescents desire privacy. Some privacy is understandable and highly recommended, but not communicating at *all* produces suspicion. A great way to honor your parents is to talk to them and communicate with them, to make them part of your life, and to make yourself part of their life. It is amazing how effective communication is in getting along with your parents. I understand that some parents are difficult. I understand that some parents can be abusive; I understand this very well. Even if your parents are difficult, this is an opportunity for you to learn how to forgive. Yes, with the guidance of your spiritual father, you need to learn how to set healthy boundaries with your parents if they are abusive, difficult, or irresponsible. This is a low percentage of parents, not a high percentage. Most parents are loving and caring. I am just addressing how to deal with difficult parents.

There is a difference between setting healthy Christian boundaries with parents, and holding on to feelings of anger and hatred toward them. Holding anger, grudges, and hatred in your heart toward them will affect you. It will hurt you. Therefore, with the guidance of your spiritual father, if your parents are very difficult or unkind, you need to learn how to set healthy Christian boundaries with them. At the same time, grasp the opportunity to learn how to forgive, and let go of anger. Also, it is an opportunity for you to pray for them and to set a Christian example. Instead of always going to bed at night angry, it is an opportunity to get on your knees and pray for them before you go to bed. Anger, grudges, and an unforgiving spirit will devour you from inside, but forgiveness will enable you to blossom and make you a true Christian.

Do Not Speak Badly to or About Them

The fifth commandment forbids injurious acts and disrespectful and unkind speech to parents. In the Book of Proverbs, we read: "The eye that mocks his father, and scorns obedience to his mother, the ravens of the valley will pick it out, and the young eagles will eat it" (Prov 30:17). You will suffer consequences if you speak badly to or about your parents. How we speak about our parents when we are together is very important: "He who curses his father or his mother shall surely be put to death" (Ex 21:17). Often, youth do not speak properly to their parents, and sometimes curse at them and say bad words to them. However, we should keep this verse before our eyes all the time. We also read: "For everyone who curses his father or his mother shall surely be put to death. He has cursed his father or his mother. His blood shall be upon him" (Lev 20:9). "Whoever curses his father or his mother, his lamp will be put out in deep darkness" (Prov 20:20). The "lamp," here, refers to good deeds. If you do all the good deeds in the world but you disrespect your parents, all your works would be like deep darkness.

Remind them that you Care

It is so easy to take one's family for granted. We think that they will always be there. However, our time with our parents is actually very short. Usually, youth leave their family home for college, then work, and not return home. Take the time to remind your parents that you love them and care about them. This is very important.

The secular world assigned days to honor our parents (Father's Day and Mother's Day). However, as Christians, we should honor them and remind them every day that we love them and care about them. I am sure that all of you spend hours every day on social media, talking and texting. What about including your parents? Greet them and send them a message of love every day to assure them that you love them and care about them.

The Blessing of Honoring Our Parents

When we honor our parents, we will receive many blessings, not only for ourselves but also for the whole nation, since it is a social matter. If all the children are obedient and respectful to their parents, the whole nation will survive and be blessed, as we read in the Book of Exodus, "Honor your father and your mother, that your days may be long upon the land which the Lord your God is giving you" (Ex 20:12). This blessing will extend from your own house to the whole nation.

Honor goes beyond words. You may say, "I love my parents," and even send them a nice gift or card on Father's Day and Mother's Day, while your attitude and behavior reveal something else. If honor is not backed up by action, it is hypocrisy; you say nice words but your actions do not reflect respect and honor. God had trouble with His children, Israel, because they honored Him with their lips, but their actions were disrespectful toward Him. They would pray, go to the temple, offer sacrifices, and keep all the rituals, but their hearts were far away from Him. Israel was continually guilty of honoring God with their lips, while their actions made Him appear worthless.

Moreover, Israel came up with some tricks to avoid honoring parents. The religious leaders—the scribes, Pharisees, and high priests—taught the people that if they decided to take the money that they were going to use to help their parents and give it to the temple as an offering to God instead, it was okay to do this and dishonor their parents and not help them (see Mk 7:10–13). They made this rule because they were greedy for money. However, the Lord Jesus Christ rebuked them, and told them that they were "making the word of God of no effect through [their] tradition" (Mk 7:13). The Lord did not approve bringing money to the temple instead of using it to help one's parents. You do have to pay your tithes, but you also have to take care of your parents. If I am planning to help my parents with some money, but I become upset with them and decide that I am going to give the money to the church instead, this is not right, and God will not accept it from you. God considered this breaking His commandment. He is the one who commanded you to take care of your parents and to honor them.

I remember in a divorce case, the husband was very angry and did not want to give any money to his wife or children. There is usually a lot of anger and frustration in any divorce. He was a rich man, and called me one day to tell me that he wanted to give all his money to the church. I asked him, "Do you want to do this in order for your wife and your children to get nothing?" He told me, *yes*; so, I refused to take his money, even for the church. I told him that we could not take this money because it belonged to his wife and children. I refused it because this was not an offering. The Lord Jesus Christ rebuked the priests for allowing this to happen.

Divorced Parents

What if one's parents are divorced and one parent speaks with their children about the other parent, and this child is now caught in the middle? Remember that the conflict is between them, not between them and you. Couples who are getting divorced usually fight for two things: children and money. They fight over who will have custody of the children because they love their children. The fact that they fight for custody means that each one wants to be in charge of his or her children because he or she loves them. Although we instruct divorced couples not to speak badly about the other spouse to their children, unfortunately, some of them do. You can listen, you can sympathize, and you can try to understand; understanding is not the same as agreeing. You can show support and compassion, but do not disrespect them. Never speak badly or negatively about them.

Cultural Obstacles to Honoring our Parents

In America, there are several factors that tend to undermine honoring parents.

    1. The impact of technology: When we feel that we have

greater expertise in technology than our parents, there is temptation for younger generations to think that their parents are outdated. In our time, a person is valued based on how much technology he knows. They say that today, illiteracy means not being technologically advanced. That is why there is a tendency to disrespect our parents. The older generation used to be respected and honored by younger generations, but, unfortunately, this is not happening currently because of the prowess of technology.

2. The rapid increase in divorce: Children are often enticed to love one parent and despise the other, as I explained, but do not fall into this trap. You need to honor both parents.

3. The tendency to blame your parents for your problems: In this society, and perhaps it is a human tendency, in general, if it is possible to blame somebody else for your problems, it is easiest and most convenient to blame our parents. Often, youth blame their parents for their problems, and because they blame them, it is difficult to honor them. Friends or people outside the family are often honored more than the parents.

The Lord Jesus Christ set an example by honoring His parents. When He was twelve years old and stayed behind in the temple, His parents went to look for Him. Once they found Him, He obeyed them and returned with them (see Lk 2:41–51). St. Luke also tells us about how the Lord Jesus Christ obeyed and submitted to His parents (see Lk 2:51). He is God and the Creator of St. Mary and St. Joseph. However, He was submissive to them because He is their Son according to the flesh, and He honored them as His parents.

In summary, you should honor your parents because:

1. It enables you to live long in the land, which is the promise.

2. It will be well with you.

3. It is the right thing to do.

4. It pleases God.

There are more reasons, but these four verses are very clear in the Holy Bible. Therefore, honoring our parents is a biblical commandment. Honoring our parents may take different forms while we are growing up, but regardless of how old we are, and even when we get into our sixties or seventies, we are required to honor our parents. One way of honoring our parents when they pass away is to remember them and pray for them, as we pray for the departed. If our parents have departed, we need to continually pray for them, and put them on our prayer list. As we pray for the living, we also pray for the departed. In the Divine Liturgy, there are some inaudible prayers, and one of the most important inaudible prayers is prayed by the priest after choosing the lamb and remembering everyone that needs to be mentioned: *Remember, O Lord, my father, my mother, my brothers, and my kin in the flesh, and my spiritual fathers. Keep those who are living, by the angel of peace, and repose those who have departed.* Thus, in every Divine Liturgy, the celebrating priest prays for his father, mother, brothers, relatives, children if he is a married priest, and for the spiritual fathers. He prays for both the living and the dead. Therefore, we are required to honor our parents regardless of our age and if they are living or departed. It is honorable before God when we honor our parents.

Many of us think that the commandment to honor parents is given to little children in order for them to be compliant and obedient, but that once we grow up, this commandment is not applicable to us. We need to re-examine our relationship with our parents. If there is any tension in this relationship, we need to try to fix things, so that the healthy family relationship will help us thrive and be good Christians.

Relationships with Siblings

The second aspect of our relationships with family members is our relationships with our siblings. We are human beings, so we expect some conflict or contention in the family, for example, between our siblings and us. In my personal opinion, dealing with siblings is a great way to prepare ourselves for other relationships, most importantly those with spouses. Dealing with siblings and with disagreements is a great school in which we learn how to deal with others and how to have successful relationships with others.

Advice

Sometimes, when you have disagreements with your siblings, you may decide not to speak to them or to avoid them in order to "have peace of mind." If you do this, when you get married and have a conflict with your spouse, you will do the same thing and this may end in divorce. However, if, right now, you learn how to work out your disagreements, compromise, and live together in harmony, this will help you deal with disagreements later in your marriage.

By dealing with your siblings, you will learn how to humble yourself by putting others before yourself, without always insisting on your own way. Sometimes, you need to put your siblings and their opinions before you, and this is a humbling experience. This is how to be like St. Mary, humble and of a lowly state, putting others before yourself.

It will also teach you how to communicate, especially when you disagree. You will learn how to communicate and discuss your differences and disagreements together. Thirdly, it will teach you to admit your faults and mistakes. All of us are human beings and we are sinners; nobody is perfect. There is nothing wrong with apologizing when you do something wrong, to tell your sibling: "I am sorry. I did this, and that was wrong. I apologize and I would like you to accept my apology." A good Christian is one who is able to admit his or her faults.

It will also teach you how to ask for forgiveness, and how to give forgiveness. Lastly and very importantly, it will teach you how to restore a relationship. When the relationship with your sibling gets really bad, what are you going to do to restore the relationship? This will help you in the future when a conflict between you and your spouse gets very difficult; the point is about how to restore a relationship instead of ending it.

Therefore, dealing with our siblings is very important because it will teach us many good lessons, such as how to humble ourselves, how to communicate, how to admit our faults, how to ask for and give forgiveness, and how to restore relationships.

Guidelines

I am going to give you guidelines about what to do when there is a conflict or sibling rivalry. When there is a conflict or disagreement between our siblings and us, there are boundaries and limits that we need to understand:

1. No hitting
2. Do not say, "I hate you." You should never say this to your brother or sister. This should not be in your dictionary, no matter what.
3. Do not boss each other. Oldest sibling tends to boss the younger ones.
4. Do not put others down or completely avoid them.

These are the four boundaries—four *do not* statements that you should always keep in mind when dealing with your siblings.

On the other hand, what *should* we do? Memorize Romans 12:10 and 12:17. "Be kindly affectionate to one another with brotherly love, in honor giving preference to one another" (Rom 12:10). "Repay no one evil for evil. Have regard for good things in the sight of all men" (Rom 12:17). If your brother or sister did something wrong to you, do not repay evil for evil; this is what the Holy Bible teaches us.

Do not fuel your competitive spirit. For example, if your parents favor one of your siblings more than you, do not ask why. This is a competitive attitude. If you have a competitive spirit, you will get into conflicts with your siblings. Look at John the Baptist when people tried to trigger jealousy in him. They told him that Jesus Christ was making more disciples than him, and that a great multitude was following Christ and leaving him. John the Baptist responded to this by saying,

"He must increase, but I must decrease" (Jn 3:30). If we say this about our siblings, we will live in peace with them. I am not saying that it is right for parents to favor my brother or sister, but even if they do, this is fine; if I accept it, let it go, and do not fuel the competitive spirit within me, I will live in peace with my siblings.

Pray for your siblings. Ask God to make them your best friends. I am sure you had friends when you were in elementary school that may live somewhere else now and with whom you no longer communicate. Who are the friends who will remain with you for the rest of your life? It is your siblings. I want your relationship with your siblings to be a friendship, and not just a regular friendship; consider them your best friends. Pray that God will engineer situations where you will have to look out for each other. God can create situations where you will need each other's help and support, and this will increase the bond between you and your siblings. Pray also that God will convict you about how you are hurting each other, when you speak negatively to each other or when you put each other down. Ask the Lord to teach you and to convict you about how you are really hurting each other.

Part V

QUESTIONS
AND ANSWERS

CHAPTER

15 Questions and Answers

15 Questions and Answers

Question: I feel like there is a lack of communication between my father of confession and me. Every time I confess, I do not feel that Abouna gives me any answers; he just listens. I feel this is wrong for me. Am I not giving him enough information? Is he teaching me silence and disciplining me by his silence? Is there a loss of communication between him and me? I am not excited about confession. I do it reluctantly. I started confessing every three months, then six months, then yearly, since I feel that he will just say, "May God forgive you," and that is it.

Answer: Did you communicate this with Abouna?

Question: No, I did not tell Abouna.

Answer: If you have not said this to Abouna, how would he know that you are upset?

Question: I thought he would know, since I am staying away from confession for long periods of time.

Answer: No, if you did not communicate this to Abouna, how would he know that you are upset about not getting any feedback? You need to communicate clearly. If something is bothering me, for example, if I am talking to you and something upsets me, I have to say it. I cannot be upset and remain upset without saying anything, and expect you to know that I am upset. I have to come to you and say, "This upsets me." It is clear that you are upset about this method, and you started refraining from confession. I advise that the next time you meet with Abouna, say, "Abouna, I honestly like to hear feedback from your reverence. I love to hear advice and comments. When you do not say anything or give me any feedback, I feel upset because I want to hear spiritual counsel. That is why I am not confessing as frequently as I should. I started coming every three months, then every six months, etc." However, be careful. I talked about "you" statements and "I" statements. You should not say, "Abouna, your way in confession is bad," or "You do not care about me." This is the "you" statement, which we need to avoid. State a fact. The fact is that he is silent. The fact is that at the end, he says, "May God forgive you." When you express what is upsetting you, this will start a very healthy dialogue between you and Abouna and will build effective communication with him.

Question: One of the points Your Grace mentioned was about not reading peoples' minds. When I am talking with my own children or with the kids in the youth group, if we get to know the kids and how they think, behave, and the way they deal with things, is this not like reading their minds? I have expectations about what is behind the questions they are asking.

Answer: Yes, there is a big difference between understanding their mindset and what they do, and reading their minds. By reading minds, I mean that you interpret what somebody means and even if he says, "I did not mean that," you still believe that this is what he meant. Then, you deal with him with this impression in your mind— that this is his intention. This is what we call "mind reading" and this is wrong. However, it is okay to say, for example, "I feel that when you do this, it might mean that. Is that right?" If he says no, believe him. If he says yes, that is good. It is okay that you understand, but you need to communicate this understanding to the person. Do not make a judgment that somebody is a certain way and even if he wants to convince you otherwise, you insist on your belief. How in the world would he convince you? This is mind reading and should be avoided.

Question: Your Grace, regarding the point about preferences versus principles, when we try to tell our children what is right and what should be done, we said that when we talk like this, we are, in effect, telling them they are not normal. Is this the right way for a father or mother to speak with their children, or how should we address issues?

Answer: When I talk about preferences, I am not talking about clear, biblical principles. For example, "Do not steal." I will not tell my son, "My preference is that you do not steal." This is a biblical principle. However, I am talking about things like the example I used, helping in household chores. Many husbands help their wives, and many do not. Some wives do not like their husbands to help and some do. This is a preference. If I deal with this as a principle, this could become problematic.

Sometimes we need to tell our children that we are different. There is a difference between saying that we are different and saying that we are abnormal. We are different because we are the children of God. "Do not be conformed to this world, but be transformed by the renewing of your mind" (Rom 12:2). We often teach them that we are unique because we are children of God. It is like the royal family in England. The royal family has certain ethics and rules that may differ from those of a common British person. In the same way, we are the royal family of God, so, we are indeed different; the way we dress, the way we speak, the way we make choices in our lives are different because we are the royal family of Christ. We are unique in this way, but we do not tell them that we are abnormal.

Question: My daughter tells me about things that happen at school and she is vague in her communication. She does not tell me the whole story, and I have to keep asking and asking. How do we train our kids, from when they are young, and assure them that when they come to us when there is a problem, we will help them solve it and not punish them? How do we get this message to our kids?

Answer: I think you are asking how we can help them understand that they need to communicate clearly and not vaguely. After you have asked several questions and understood the whole story, you can tell her, "In general, it is better for you to speak in a structured way. For example, with this story, if you had started from the beginning, it would have been clear. However, listen to how you said it (and then repeat it to her). This could have made me understand it in a different way." Have a small workshop with her about this story, about how she communicated it to you, and how you expect her to communicate with you. After you finish the workshop, you can tell her, "Okay, now tell me the same story in this structured way." In this way, you are training her. This does not only apply to stories from school, but also if she tells you a story from Sunday school, for example. When you ask her what she learned in Sunday school, if you feel that she is being vague, tell her, "No. I understand this story because I already know it, but try to be structured. Try to use strategic ways to explain the story so the listener can understand." With practice, she will be able to express herself directly and clearly.

Question: Of course, we should not get mad at them in the end.

Answer: No, you should not get mad at her. As we said, we need to consider the age and maturity of the children. Of course, I am not expecting a young child to communicate in the same way as an adult.

Question: If I say that something is my preference and the children do not agree with it, what should I do? It is still something very important. They are old enough and I do not want to force them, but if I kept repeating that this is my preference and they still feel that it is not their preference, our preferences will now interfere. As a mother, I feel that something is a preference and the children respect it, but they insist, "You are from a different generation and tradition. We respect your preference, but we will not follow it." For me, it is very important for them to follow it because, like Your Grace said, we are Christians and we have certain ways. Should I insist and make it a principle, or should I just leave them until they make it a principle?

Answer: There are several points to this question. First, is it truly a preference or is it a principle? Preferences, in general, can be compromised; principles cannot be compromised. If it is a preference and it will not hurt them if you compromise it, we need to negotiate with our children, so they do not feel that Mom and Dad always say no. If it is something that will not hurt them and does not contradict with biblical teaching, it is okay if the other person is not willing to accept the other's preference.

The second point is the age of the children. Very young children are still immature, so you need to teach them obedience and give them room to develop their own personalities and make their own decisions. Teach them how to make right decisions. Sometimes a fight may occur between a mother and her young daughter about which dress she will wear on Sunday to church. The dress the girl wants to wear could be nice and appropriate for church, but the mother wants her to wear something different. They keep arguing and create a problem. The mother is actually canceling her daughter's personality. Why does she not just encourage her daughter and tell her the dress is nice?

Question: What if it is inappropriate?

Answer: I am saying that if it is appropriate, the mother should not be stubborn. If it is not appropriate, this is not a preference, but a principle because now we are talking about worshipping God and how to be dressed appropriately when going to church.

Age is important. Parents should teach young children obedience and critical thinking skills like how to make decisions and how to make good choices. With teenagers, there should be discussions and parents need to convince them of the right thing to do. If I force a teenager, he could rebel against me. We need to convince them and have them do the right thing while they are convinced, not just because they are forced to comply.

Therefore, is it a preference or a principle? If it is a preference, parents should compromise. There is nothing wrong with that. God was willing to compromise with Abraham (see Gen 18:16–33). Sometimes, parents feel if they say something and their children challenge it and the parents change their minds, this is a weakness. No, it is not.

Question: What about if it is something like helping around the house? He does not want to help but I need him to help. It is not a principle, but it is still very important.

Answer: No, that is a principle. A son should share and do his duty. He should be responsible. However, there is still the question of age. We need to know if the expectation is realistic for the age.

Question: If it is realistic, I should insist?

Answer: Yes, convince, talk, and train until they reach it.

Question: One of the biggest problems for us is to figure out what is important and requires insistence, as principles, and what we can compromise. Sometimes, we have difficulty compromising. This sometimes creates major issues when we deal with our kids. We may not allow them things that are not major concerns because we do not want them to get into the habit that this is okay. We may sometimes stop them from doing things that are not serious, but in the fear that they will continue to take yes forever or as a habit, or we know that if they get hooked on these things, it may lead to other things.

Answer: As you are afraid for kids to take yes forever, my advice to the parents is do not say no forever. Sometimes, parents say no to everything that is asked of them. When will your child hear yes? Extremes are wrong. If parents want to please their children and says yes to everything, this will spoil the children and make them irresponsible. The parents who say no to everything is a controlling father or mother and the children will become rebellious. They will rebel against their parents' authority. Balance is good; sometimes I say yes, and sometimes I say no. This also presents a practical image of God, because although He hears our prayers, sometimes he says yes and sometimes no, but always for what is best for us.

Also, a piece of advice for you with your children is to never get into a power struggle with them. Avoid power struggles as much as you can. If you get into a power struggle and the child disobeys your word and does his own thing, it is over. As soon as you feel that it will end in a power struggle, it is better to compromise and keep your authority in the family rather than let him challenge your authority. Once he rebels against your authority, that is it. Your authority is gone.

Question: If I ask for something, it loses its value and meaning to me. At the same time, I get upset when my husband does not understand on his own what I want, without me saying it. What do you advise?

Answer: The problem here lies in the belief system. It is a problem when one's belief system, i.e., personal beliefs and assumptions, are not functional. She [the speaker] is making a statement here: "When I ask for something it loses its value and meaning." That is a belief system; that is one of her beliefs. This belief needs to change, and she needs to understand that when she asks for something, this does not make it lose value or meaning since she different from the other person. The other person may not know what her needs are.

It is clear that this belief is not working for you; it is upsetting and your husband does not know why. In general, if you find that a belief like this does not work for you or make you happy, you need to change it, especially if it is not a biblical belief or doctrine. This belief is not biblical, because although God knows all our needs and can gives us more than we ask for even before we ask, God encourages us to ask. "For everyone who asks receives, and he who seeks finds, and to him who knocks it will be opened" (Mt 7:8). God encourages us to express our needs.

Question: Sometimes, the way I communicate becomes part of my character. It is not easy to change my character in order to better communicate. How can I do this?

Answer: This is true. If someone always communicates in an aggressive way, he becomes an aggressive person. Yes, it is not easy, but it is also not impossible. First, be convinced that you need to change your character and the way you communicate. Second, ask for the grace of God to help you because without the grace of God, you cannot achieve anything. Third, try to practice, especially with the people who love and support you. Try to practice changing the way you communicate, and listen to the feedback from others. Fourth, have patience and hope that one day you will change. When you change your character and the way you communicate, you will be happy, and this is what we call the process of transformation. This is what St. Paul says about being transformed by the renewal of your mind; it starts here. You need to renew your mind to understand what better communication is, what the character of the children of God is—this is renewal of mind. Then, start working on it. You will be able to achieve it through the grace of God. I agree that it is not easy, but it is not impossible. It is possible. "I can do all things through Christ who strengthens me" (Phil 4:13).

Question: I think that friendship after marriage is very difficult because with friendship, the results of a problem only affect one side. The other friend listens and gives advice, but the end result will not affect him. In marriage, issues always affect both sides. This is why both are worried and there can be a lot of tension. In this situation, it is not easy to apply friendship to a married couple.

Answer: I agree with you that when a friend has an issue, the outcome will not affect the other, and that in marriage, the outcome will affect both spouses. However, let us look at it in a different way. If there are conflicts and arguments in marriage, can both spouses reach a desirable outcome? Absolutely not. If a husband insists on his opinion and his advice regarding how to solve a problem, and his wife tells him that she will not do what he says and they get into a fight, will this method enrich their marriage? The answer is no. There are two scenarios: He can support her needs, and give her space to try her solutions or her ideas. When he gives her his opinion, he does not do so in a controlling or aggressive way but in a convincing way. Imposing his opinion may create rebellion, and she will do what she wants. The outcome of the problem will not change. Additionally, a conflict occurred in the family and there was a break down in the relationship.

Question: In my opinion, this is how our culture is. We are used to always having one decision-maker in the family. There is one person who has more responsibility than the other. I feel that this is the reason for having these kinds of conflicts or this kind of relationship. One spouse says, "This is the way I see it. This is the way we are used to solving this kind of problem, and you have to listen." I guess it is something we have to change in our culture. It is not easy.

Answer: We need to talk to each other, understand one another, and listen to the other's opinion. In situations like the example I gave about the wife having a problem at work, she understands her work atmosphere better than anyone else. We should trust the other person's opinion, perception, and ability to solve a problem, and be encouraging. If a mistake happens, it is okay; it is not the end of the world. Many people learn from their mistakes. We often tell priests to give servants the freedom to act, and if they make a mistake, it is okay. There is always the opportunity to learn and to fix mistakes.

Question: My son is in his early teens. He tends to say the partial truth. I feel that I am largely to blame for that. What is your advice on how to address this huge issue?

Answer: I am glad that you addressed this and said, "I am largely to blame for that." You are aware that there is some sort of miscommunication or lack of trust, which causes your son to share partial truths. You need to work on this, rebuild trust, create a safe atmosphere, and build a friendship with your son, so that he feels comfortable to uncover and share the whole truth without the fear of being rejected or severely punished (punished not in proportion to the problem). Do not misunderstand me—I am not telling you not to discipline your children. You need to discipline them. However, discipline should be in proportion to the problem and it must be communicated that it is done out of love: "I am disciplining you because I love you." "For whom the Lord loves He chastens" (Heb 12:6).

Question: Can we consider other family members, such as in-laws, a barrier to communication, especially when they always interfere in everything in our life, and my future spouse always lets them interfere in our problems?

Answer: You are right. Feeling that the final decision should come from the in-laws is a barrier in communication. That is why, in marriage, we tell the husband, "A man shall leave his father and mother and be joined to his wife" (Gen 2:24), and we tell the wife, "Forget your own people also, and your father's house" (Ps 45:10). The words forget and leave do not mean to dishonor them, but refer to creating healthy boundaries. Interference from in-laws often creates major problems between the couple. Many times, instead of blaming the in-laws, we blame the spouse who asks them to interfere. This is wrong. The reason for this could be that there is not much trust between the spouses. If you do not trust your spouse, how did you agree to marry him or her? Before making the final decision to get married, you need to trust the other person. If you do not trust him and still trust your parents more, do not get married.

Question: Sometimes, their opinion is right. The couple may still be at the beginning of their life, and the in-laws can guide them correctly.

Answer: What you are saying is accurate. Perhaps in all situations, their opinion is correct because of their experiences and other things. However, sometimes just because it comes from them, it makes the other spouse defensive. That is why it is better to have the mediator be the priest, the father of confession of both spouses. Here, the advice will be more acceptable. Or, if we want to ask them, one spouse should not be asking his parents and then bringing back the answer, but they should agree together that they will ask together. In this way, both of them are ready to ask and get advice. If advice is given, even if it is correct, but the other spouse is not willing to accept it, it will cause a problem rather than resolve a situation.

Question: When there are no questions, it does not mean that the message was clear. The listener may be embarrassed or not trained to talk, discuss, and question.

Answer: Yes, many people are embarrassed and very shy to speak in a public meeting such as this. However, as we discussed, there are many methods of communication. For example, you wrote your question on a piece of paper, so that is one way to communicate. Or, if you want to ask a question orally but you are nervous to do so, at the beginning you can say that you are shy or embarrassed. Saying this will eliminate anxiety and you will be able to express yourself and share.

Question: How do I communicate to my son that eating too much is harmful to his health? He has started hiding food and eating behind my back.

Answer: My opinion is that you should discuss this issue calmly with your son. It may not be a real problem. Perhaps he is an adolescent, going through a growth spurt, and needs to eat a lot. Teenagers are growing and their bodies are building muscle, so they need to eat more. It may be normal. Do not judge it as wrong, but discuss it with him and find out the reason. If he is older, it may be something psychological, but this occurs more frequently with girls. If he is obese, you need to discuss further with his physician.

Question: When one spouse talks about something and the other responds concerning a different issue, and at the end says that this is the extent of his ability to understand, what should I do in order to get him to deal with the issue at hand?

Answer: Some people have selective understanding. When you talk about something specific, he does not understand. When you talk about something else, he understands very well. You need to see if this is selective understanding, or if he really has a problem and misunderstands everything. If he truly misunderstands everything, this is what his mental ability is like. However, if he has selective understanding, this is a type of manipulation and avoidance, and you need to confront him. A third possible reason is that you may not be communicating clearly.

Question: My oldest son is very argumentative, especially with his brother. He is usually very good and has a good point to convey, but sometimes, when I watch him, he just wants to win the argument and make his listener feel bad. How can I help?

Answer: This is true. Many people go into arguments and debates thinking about how to win, especially because they learn to debate in schools. As a parent, you may need to do a Bible study about how to speak in order to give grace to the listener. Bring to his attention that every time he speaks to the other person, his brother, he can make it a point to make that person feel good. Every time he does so, reward this behavior, until it becomes natural. In this way, you help him eliminate his negative behavior and train him to speak gracefully.

Question: Isn't the purpose of having an argument to tell the other person that you are right?

Answer: There is a difference between dialogue for the purpose of understanding the other person's point of view and sharing my point of view, and competitive arguments, such as the presidential debates. The goal is to win the point and put the other person down. This is not a good way to dialogue. We need to teach our children to always let their words be "seasoned with salt" (Col 4:6) in order to "impart grace to the hearers" (Eph 4:29), not to make the listener feel bad. The question says that her son wants to make the listener feel bad; this does not conform with the biblical teaching to give grace to the listener.

Question: I have three boys ages 13–17. How safe is it to speak to them about love or sex? Can we open up these subjects in order to educate them, or is it not advised?

Answer: It is definitely advised to discuss these subjects because if you do not educate them, they will learn elsewhere.

Question: When I get mad at my husband about a certain issue, I keep silent and do not speak to him for two days, or more, until I am able to talk about it. Is that right?

Answer: There is a difference between holding a grudge and not being ready to discuss a certain issue. If you keep silent and do not talk at all, of course this is not right. Perhaps you can say that you are not ready to talk about this specific issue, and ask him to give you three or four days, or even one week, until you are ready to talk about it. However, you need to communicate as husband and wife. Not talking at all is unhealthy for the relationship, so it is not right.

Question: In the example you gave about the husband who does not share the financial accounts with his wife [see page 52], he may have another reason for not showing her. Perhaps she thinks that he does not have good financial management, so it would be like a vicious cycle. What could someone give up in order to earn trust in a situation like that?

Answer: I think things will be resolved once they are brought out in the open and discussed together. For example, if she thinks that he is not managing their money wisely, this issue needs to be discussed. If he really does not manage money wisely, this needs to be discussed and resolved. However, the solution is not for her to hide the financial statements from him since he does not manage money wisely. As it is said, two wrongs do not make a right. This would be escalation. This vicious cycle can be interrupted by open, honest communication and by trying to resolve the conflict together.

Question: How can you stop scorekeeping?

Answer: There is a difference between remembering what happened and holding these things against the other person. Some people have a good memory and that, in itself, is not a negative thing and should not work against them, as long as the person is not keeping grudges in his heart or holding these memories and events of the past against the other. Therefore, if I remember what happened, this is related to memory. On the other hand, we can stop scorekeeping by acquiring a forgiving heart. We should always remind ourselves that if God were to keep score for us, who could stand before Him? "If You, Lord, should mark iniquities [that is scorekeeping], O Lord, who could stand?" (Ps 129:3). If you want God to keep score for you, keep score for the other. If you want Him to forget your scores, you have to forgive others. Acquire a forgiving heart and you will stop keeping score.

Usually, when there is repetitive behavior, that is when the other person starts to keep score. However, let me challenge this by asking, "Does keeping score stop the repetitive behavior?" If it does not, then it is not wise to keep doing more of the same. That is not healthy. If I gave someone medicine and he did not improve, it is not wise to keep giving him the same medicine over and over again. I should try to think about alternative solutions.

Question: Why do they keep score of the bad things and not the good things?

Answer: That is another exercise. If you want to keep score, keep score of the good things.

Question: Is it wrong to work harder for the first couple of years after you graduate?

Answer: As long as you maintain balance in your life, and if working hard would not be at the expense of other things, such as your spiritual life, your health, your social life, your service, your family life, then it is better to work hard so that when you get married, you can slow down a little bit. Before getting married, you have less responsibility. If you work hard during this time, it is okay, as long as it is not at the expense of other areas in your life.

Question: Does the Church promote one spouse staying home and raising the kids?

Answer: In the Holy Bible, both parents work. If you read Proverbs 31 about the virtuous woman, she was working and helping her husband. "She seeks wool and flax, and willingly works with her hands. She is like the merchant ships, she brings her food from afar. She also rises while it is yet night, and provides food for her household, and a portion for her maidservants. She considers a field and buys it; from her profits she plants a vineyard. She girds herself with strength, and strengthens her arms. She perceives that her merchandise is good, and her lamp does not go out by night" (Prov 31:13–18). What does it mean that her lamp does not go out by night? She is working night and day; she is helping.

We promote having a balanced life, not overworking. I know many mothers do not work until their children go to school, and after they go to school, they work part time. When the children come home, they find their mother waiting for them; they do not go into empty homes. They have a balance in life.

Question: Many fathers are always at work and do not have time. They do not devote much time to the family, and they justify it by saying that they are working for the family.

Answer: If they work 40 hours per week, which is full time, they can make time for their families. The problem is that some fathers want to work more than 40 hours, maybe 80 hours, and that is when problems arise. If it is a requirement for their job that, for example, they have to go in at night when they call them, they cannot get out of that.

Question: Many wives say that their relationship with their husband started out great, but then the husband, one way or another, forced them to disrespect him. What is the solution to this?

Answer: The solution is that the commandments in the Crowning Ceremony are unconditional. His love for her is unconditional. He cannot say, "I stopped loving her because she does not respect me." It is the same for her. Her respect for him should be unconditional. Any commandment is unconditional.

Also, if she stops respecting him because of something he did, does this solve the problem? Or, does it worsen the problem? Of course, it does not solve the problem, but complicates it. The third point is that nobody said that she should not talk about what hurts or bothers her. However, discuss it respectfully. Saying, "I cannot respect him because he changed," is not right. I maintain my respect for him and respectfully discuss how he has changed. There will be better results if issues are discussed respectfully. Disrespecting him will produce no results or negative results.

Question: How can you have a relationship of true unity if you are not really equal, if the woman has to be submissive to the man? That is inequality.

Answer: Submission is not against equality. God the Son and God the Father are equal, but in Gethsemane, the Lord Jesus Christ said, "Nevertheless, not as I will, but as You will" (Mt 26:39). That is submission. We are confused in thinking that submission is against equality. It is not, since it is willful submission—i.e., submission out of love. It is not forced submission. It is not the submission of a slave to a master. It is the submission of the Church to her beloved Bridegroom.

Question: Equality is an organizational problem. You cannot have two captains on a ship. Also, a 50/50 partnership is one of the most dangerous business organizations because if you encounter problems, no one can say no. Equality in an organization is fine when everything is going well, but not when there are issues.

Answer: When we speak about equality, we are speaking about equality of essence, of value, and not in function. You are speaking about function, the administrative role. Functions are different.

However, the price of a male is the Blood of our Lord Jesus Christ. The price of a female is the Blood of our Lord Jesus Christ. In this respect, they are equal, as children of God. As St. Paul says, "There is neither Jew nor Greek, there is neither slave nor free, there is neither male nor female; for you are all one in Christ Jesus" (Gal 3:28).

When you speak about function, it is true that we cannot have two captains on a ship. For example, we do not have two brains in our body. If there were two brains, the person would die. The best metaphor for man and woman is the brain and heart in a human body; both of them are equally important. You cannot live without either one of them. The heart submits to the brain, because the brain controls the heart by sending nerve impulses, while the heart nurtures the brain with the blood supply. If the heart decided not to be submissive to the brain and to start working on its own, this would result in cardiac fibrillation and death. In the same way, if there is not enough blood going from the heart to the brain, there will be thrombus, paralysis, and perhaps death.

Question: The word "submission" causes some fear. Is there a better word to use?

Answer: I do not know a better word; this is the word in the Holy Bible. Fear comes when it is submission of slavery. However, it is willful submission, submission of love. It is submission as a response of love. The Church submits because it feels the love of the Lord Jesus Christ. It is like a circle. Love leads to submission and submission leads to love. They feed each other. Also, love from the husband contains in itself humility, and humility can accept opinions and ideas from the other person. The husband's humility makes him receptive to his wife. We say, "As Sarah obeyed Abraham," but Abraham also listened to Sarah many times. Moreover, God defended Sarah and told Abraham, "Whatever Sarah has said to you, listen to her voice" (Gen 21:12). As we say, if the husband is the head; a head has two ears and one tongue. This means he should listen twice as much as he speaks.

Question: If submission is for the female and love for the male, why can't both of them do both things?

Answer: They work together in harmony. The brain is able to function correctly if it receives enough blood from the heart. If the brain does not receive enough blood from the heart, it cannot function correctly. By her emotions, nurture, and support, she will help the husband make right decisions. When the brain sends impulses to the heart, that is its responsibility. Why is it not the opposite? Well, why does the ear not see and the eye not hear? That is how God, the Manufacturer, designed and planned the family. God created the man in order to be in charge, to be a leader, to lead the family in the way of righteousness and godliness. God created the woman in order to provide nurture, love, and support to the family. That is how the family will function correctly. If the brain is not functioning correctly, you will seek a neurosurgeon. In the same way, if the husband is not functioning correctly, you take him to Abouna.

Question: What is the view of Holy Scripture on the husband and wife's relationship versus the way parents treat children? Are they supposed to sacrifice more for the children than for each other? Sometimes, they get more focused on the children.

Answer: If the husband and wife do not have a good relationship, if the marital relationship is not strong, if they are not one in spirit, flesh, and soul, they cannot have godly offspring. In the Book of Malachi, we read about why God made them one: "But did He not make them one, having a remnant of the Spirit? And why one? He seeks godly offspring" (Mal 2:15). Godly offspring can only come from a strong marital relationship. If you are only focusing on your children, and not on the marital relationship, you are wasting our time.

Question: What can we do if one spouse is more spiritual than the other?

Answer: The question here becomes, does the one who is more spiritual think that he or she is better than the other? If I am more spiritual than the other person and I feel than I am better, this is the real problem, because there is judgment here. However, if I am concerned about my spouse's salvation and eternal life, and it is not because I feel that I am better, then I will know how to handle this and bring his spiritual life up. How so? If I feel than I am better than him, this will be expressed even in my tone of voice and how I address conflict. I will accuse him of not going to church. It would be as if I were Abouna to him. On the other hand, if I am concerned about his eternal life, the person who is more spiritual needs to remember four things: Love "bears all things, believes all things, hopes all things, endures all things" (1 Cor 13:7). If I am more spiritually mature, then I should at least endure everything and hope for everything, and then, there will be no problem. I will spend time, like St. Monica who spent time in her own inner room praying for her son [St. Augustine] and asking God to change his life.

Also, by demonstrating my spirituality, by my example, I can change him. That is what St. Peter says, "Wives, likewise, be submissive to your own husbands, that even if some do not obey the word, they, without a word, may be won by the conduct of their wives, when they observe your chaste conduct accompanied by fear" (1 Pet 3:1–2). When I demonstrate my spirituality, not by my words but by my behavior, I will win my husband over. However, if I boss him around as if I were his priest, judge him, condemn him, and tell him what to do, he would say, "You go to church all the time, but it has not done anything to improve you."

Therefore, the person who feels that he is more spiritual should ask himself this question: "Do I feel that I am better than my spouse?" If the answer is yes, then you are the one who has the problem, not the other person. Feeling that you are better is very destructive to any relationship.

Question: If you will be rewarded on earth for honoring your parents, is there also a heavenly reward for honoring them? Or is it just an earthly reward?

Answer: You will have both an earthly reward and a heavenly reward.

Question: What are the things that you should follow if your parents ask you to do them?

Answer: St. Paul says to obey your parents in the Lord. When they advise you in the Lord, you should follow them, no matter what. However, when it comes to your opinion, for example, if you do not like that they ask you to be home by 9:00 p.m. and you start arguing with them, this is against honoring your parents, since honoring your parents means to value their advice. If they tell you that you need to be home by 9:00, you need to be home at 9:00.

Question: Is it wrong to tell them that you do not want to be home by 9:00?

Answer: You are not allowed to argue, but you are allowed to discuss. There is a big difference between an argument and a discussion. Arguing means that you are going to continue to argue until you get what you want, and this is not obedience. However, you can have a discussion, meaning that if you have some points that you want to explain, you will explain it to them, but after this, you will abide by whatever they tell you.

Question: Should you break your fast if your parents tell you to do so, if you are sick?

Answer: If you are sick, you can get absolution from your priest, then you can break your fast, and it depends on the kind of sickness. If your parents ask you to break the fast, you may kindly tell them that you will call Abouna first and see what he advises. If Abouna gives you absolution, then you can break your fast.

Question: Am I honoring them if I go to someone higher than them to ask him about something they said?

Answer: Yes, that someone is a priest in the church, because God gave the priests authority to give absolution. Your parents cannot absolve you to break a fast. You need to get this absolution from a person who has the authority. For example, if you need to get antibiotics and your parents are not physicians, and you go to a physician because he has the authority to prescribe this antibiotic for you, are you dishonoring them because you went to a person who has that authority? Of course not.

Question: Can you give us an example of what not to follow them in?

Answer: Follow them in what they do right. Regarding what they do wrong, you need to forgive them and pray for them. That is why one of the points about honoring them is to forgive their failings. I am putting into consideration that no parents in the world are a perfect example.

Glory be to God, forever. Amen.

Lightning Source UK Ltd.
Milton Keynes UK
UKHW040950251022
411061UK00001B/77